Creative Gardeners

Creative Gardeners

Douglas Ellory Pett

Alison Hodge

Douglas Ellory Pett, 1924–2005

Creative Gardeners is published in memory of the author, who died just before its publication. 'Through his books and articles, Douglas Pett made a major contribution to the field of garden history in Cornwall and beyond.'
(Roger Trenoweth, Editor of *The Cornish Garden*, in the *West Briton*, 3 March 2005)

Contents

Introduction

This is a book for gardeners about gardens. Twenty private gardens have been selected which have been designed and, for the most part, brought into existence by their owners. They have been chosen for their diversity, creativity, and their skill in cultivation.

The gardens range from a former marsh, to moors and open upland; from frost pockets to areas of excessive rainfall. Some have had the advantage of previous cultivation, while others have been wrung from raw fields, or even literally hewn out of the valley slopes. Consequently, whether you garden in a town or suburb, or have extensive grounds, there will be some community of interest to be found among this selection.

All of the owners volunteered, or in response to my questioning confessed that their garden reflected their own personality. On the one occasion that I was foolish, or perhaps impertinent enough to ask, 'What sort of personality might this be?', I was swiftly answered, 'Well, look around you!' So this became the central theme of this book. I have endeavoured in the descriptions, based on conversations with the owners, to convey aspects of their individuality, which together with the illustrations will offer readers the opportunity, as it were, to 'look around' for themselves.

This is a book about gardens and not about plants. Of course, there would not be a garden without plants, but I have mentioned them in my descriptions only in a general way, as being characteristic, or perhaps of special interest.

My title is *Creative Gardeners*, but it will soon become evident that they are all in Cornwall, although I must hasten to add that this does not mean that they are therefore distinctively Cornish. On the contrary, even

those who are themselves Cornish, and they are the minority, did not see their gardens as essentially Cornish. 'You do what you can with what you have got,' explained one owner, and this exactly expresses the position of every gardener. All of the conditions in these particular gardens will be found somewhere else in the British Isles, and most of the problems faced are universal.

All except three of the gardens are currently open to the public, but since this is not a guidebook only general notes on opening have been given. Full details of these and all the open gardens in Cornwall, with illustrations, will be found in my book *The Cornwall Gardens Guide*. Most also appear in the National Gardens Scheme 'Yellow Book', or the annual leaflet issued by the Cornwall Tourist Board.

It is usual at this point to continue with a list of acknowledgements, but in this case my thanks must go almost entirely to the owners of the gardens themselves for putting up with my inquisitiveness, and the inconvenience caused by photographing. More than this we were touched by the welcome we were given, and the hospitality we received. Although compiling this work has required a great deal of effort, this has been fully rewarded by the many interesting people we have met, and the fascinating gardens we have seen.

I must not end, however, without giving testimony to the help I have received from my wife Mary, who has driven me about, remembered what I ought not to have forgotten, and generally kept me up to scratch, without whom this work might never have been completed.

Douglas Ellory Pett
Tresillian, Truro, 2005

Bonython is an ancient manor dating from at least 1277, when it was lived in by a family of the same name. The area around the house had been planted in 1830 by Treseders' historic Truro nursery, who were engaged again in 1961 to landscape the walled 'Pleasure Gardens', neglected during the Second World War.

When Richard and Sue Nathan from South Africa came here in 2000, both the walled garden and the surrounding landscape were again beginning to show their age, and in dire need of rejuvenation. Sue, who took over the management of the garden, first sought the advice of Charles Williams of the Burncoose Nursery, the successor of Treseders in landscaping, who suggested the planting of twenty ornamental trees, and the restoration of a second lake. The trees having been selected, the work of digging out the lake was put in hand, raising banks on each side. This was to be Sue's first essay in creating a new South African garden. Impressed by the sight of ornamental grasses in another garden, she decided to create 'hot' beds by massed plantings of grasses on each of the long sides of the lake, with multicoloured cannas on the top of the higher, south-facing bank. These dazzling beds have been designed to be reflected by the lake in a most spectacular fashion (right), which is nothing less than inspirational. At the east end a gravel bed has been laid out which is to be the home of proteas, leucodendrons, and other similar exotic plants (page 10). A place has been found in the rill joining the new lake to the old 'Lake Joy', named after the wife of a former owner, for the damp-loving restios (pages 10–11). This new lake has been aptly christened 'Lake Sue'.

Bonython Estate Garden

Introducing South African plants

The woodlands to the west have been planted with tree ferns (left), leading on to the picturesque 'Quarry Lake' from which stone had been taken for use on the estate. The naturalistic atmosphere of this eerie place is to be preserved.

In contrast to this new South African garden, it was decided to retain the walled Pleasure and Vegetable Gardens as traditionally English. They were both in need of complete refurbishment. With the help of John Moreland, a Penzance designer, a plan was drawn up. In the first garden there was a discontinuity between the levels of the swimming pool and the lawn, which was to be disguised by a long bed of rambling catmint with tall matching alliums. This at once introduced a swathe of colour the length of the garden. At the entrance, which is at a little distance from the house itself, a simple parterre, edged with golden box, was laid out with a vista through an arch to a stone seat as a focal point at the end of the lawn. Here again, as in the long pool bed, the parterre was planted *en masse* with large white tulips, creating an instant visual impact in the spring by simple means.

The Vegetable Garden had been separated by a hedge, which was cut through to open a long view down the pool bed, into the Vegetable Garden, which was now laid out as a potager, through a gate on to the sloping lawn leading down to Lake Joy. Although the potager is a working area, the ornamental

vegetables and drifts of cutting flowers are a fine sight in summer (top left). On passing through the gate a thatched hut is seen, which is intended as a refreshment shelter for visitors. The lawn beyond had already been planted with fruit trees, including some old Cornish varieties – among them Ben's Red, Scilly Pearl and Pear Apple – around which brick-edged beds have been cut in which seed of wild flowers gathered from the Kirstenbosch have been planted, with the intention of creating a gradual transition between the peaceful English garden, and the radiant lake and hot garden.

John Julius Norwich has described Bonython (below left) as 'an exceptionally elegant house', but like so many late-eighteenth-century rebuilds, the rear is undistinguished and best not seen. Here the Nathans have added a one-storey, L-shaped wing, forming a courtyard bounded on three sides. This at once provided Sue with an opportunity to design an impressive water-garden (right). In the centre is a cubic granite tank where the smooth, reflectant water weeps over the edges. The channels of clear water with slate-coloured depths alternate with square surrounding walks planted with a rim of alternating grasses – *Stipa gigantica* and *Imperata cylindrica* 'Rubra'. Along the house, a raised bed is planted with foliage plants, while large red pots with restios are ranged

along the adjacent wall. The east wing has a pergola from which hang grape vines, under which are loungers, chairs and tables to recline in the sun. This basically simple, though effective design has been recognized by those who have seen it as having a distinctly South African feel. From the open side, up steps and across a lawn, can be seen in season a wholly Cornish planting of rhododendrons and azaleas in the Cider Press Garden (mid left).

This first garden in our selection is beyond the size or scope of the majority of gardeners, but it has a relevance in this context, since like two other similarly large gardens it is the result of the single-minded determination of a practical gardener. This is a remarkable example, over a period of a mere five years, of the much maligned 'instant' gardening, but the principles involved are applicable in any garden needing quickly to be brought to life again – that is that the planting should be simple, and if it works should be repeated *en masse* for the maximum effect.

Sue Nathan remarked during our conversations, 'Every plant you see, I have planted!' She continued, 'I have put so much of myself into the garden, and it has given me so much joy, that I want to share it with others.' It is, therefore, open from Tuesdays to Fridays through April to September, but the weekends are kept as 'home days'.

Bosvigo is probably the best known of all the gardens in this book, since it has been televised, and appears on a videotape and in many books and journals. Michael and Wendy Perry came here in 1969, when the Georgian house was disfigured by a monstrous Victorian wing. After much deliberation the planners allowed this to be demolished in 1979, with the exception of the conservatory, which now stands isolated as a greenhouse (right), in which tender and houseplants are grown. The walls of the first garden were then built out of stone from this demolished wing, to form a secluded and sheltered garden for private use.

The site has been inhabited since before 1280, and is characteristic of early Cornish dwellings in being tucked into the side of a hill, protected from the north, where the prevailing south-westerly winds blow over the top. This accommodation to comfortable ancient living, centuries later, makes an admirable site for a garden, which is open only to the rarer easterlies. The soil, however, is thin and shaley, and so requires regular mulching by the application of spent mushroom compost. Although this might raise the pH of the slighty acid soil, this is to the advantage of herbaceous plants, which are the most commonly grown. Only a few azaleas and rhododendrons have been planted, usually as specialities, such as *Rhododendron fragrantissimum*, which, as its name suggests, is sweetly scented.

When the Perrys arrived the woodland that now forms a contrast to the more formal gardens around the house was an impenetrable jungle of Portuguese laurel and young sycamores. The arrival of Dutch Elm Disease in 1976 necessitated the whole woodland being felled, but the soil proved hard

Bosvigo

Associating plant colour and form

and stony, so that at first nothing could be planted without digging a pocket to fill with good earth. The problem was compounded by the lack of shelter, so that it was some time before it became possible to cultivate it successfully.

The design and planting of the gardens, for which Bosvigo is celebrated, has been the inspiration of Wendy Perry, who had been trained as an artist. But it was her own instinct for colour, rather than theory, which is reflected in the planting. She likes to work with a palette restricted perhaps to only two colours, as is seen in the White and Yellow Garden. Similar colours or textures may be repeated in a bed, rather like *leit motifs* or themes in a musical composition. Since the colour schemes are summer flowering, the White and Yellow Garden has been given a more permanent framework, with paths quartering the garden and clipped yellow privet as accent plants.

The adjoining walled garden (far left and above) follows a quite different pattern, but again restricted, in this case to blue, mauve and purple. A 'hot border' however, bursts into flower in the woodland in late summer with deep-coloured dahlias (left), but here contrasted with yellow.

Wendy has principally been influenced by the classic writers, Rosemary Verey, whose dictum that 'a garden should curtsey to the house' is nowhere better exemplified

than here, and Margery Fish. However, one garden in particular has been an inspiration to her – that of Peter Healing at The Priory, Kemerton, near Tewkesbury, where in a long border the colours have been evenly graded from pastel to bright shades and back again. A small red bed, with stalks and leaves as well as flowers all red, also made a deep impression.

Once the new shelter trees had grown sufficiently, the woodland could be developed, with acers and other ornamental trees underplanted with a carpet especially of hellebores, narcissus and other 'little treasures' too numerous to mention (above). Here Michael has been in his element, snaking paths beneath the canopy of leaves. The courtyards behind the house have offered the opportunity for more architectural plants. Shaped topiary shrubs in tubs (right) can be moved about, and the raised beds in shade planted with ferns and other striking foliage plants. Other pots are brought out when in season, like the spectacular flowering Oriental lily 'Casablanca', only to be discreetly hidden away a week or two later.

Visitors have often remarked on the neatness of the beds, with no bare patches as can so easily happen with herbaceous plants with a limited flowering or lifespan. This problem has been solved by a long and careful selection of varieties, aided by the fruits of experience. For instance, a second white flower would be planted to rise up and take over from another which is in decline. Continued vigilance is necessary to deadhead, and sometimes plant replacements throughout the summer. The gorgeous Oriental poppy, for example, will leave a conspicuous gap when it ceases flowering. It is then cut down to the ground, and later-flowering species planted around the stump. Annuals, such as cosmos or cerinthe, may be introduced to fill spaces and prolong the sequence, being disposed of during the splitting and replanting of the herbaceous varieties in the winter. Such practices will not recommend themselves to the indifferent or idle gardener!

Another of the influential features of Bosvigo has been the nursery, by which the more unusual varieties seen in the garden have become widely distributed. Originally this came about as a side product of the need to split herbaceous varieties every three years, or even annually. This at first produced many new plants which could be used in other parts of the garden. But then, as time went by, there came a surplus to give to one's friends, or sell on a table on open days. Eventually, as quantity and demand grew, a nursery was set up on an old tennis court, and a catalogue was printed, which tends to vary according to the three-yearly rotation of the splitting. There has also been an attempt, with some success, to raise a variety of hellebore that does not demurely hang its head.

Bosvigo is open to visitors on Thursdays and Fridays, usually from the beginning of March to the end of September.

The intriguing garden at Caervallack is one of the most original in this book, not least because it is the inspiration of two artists. Mathew Robinson and Louise McClary had together, in advance, drawn a picture of their 'dream house', and eventually in 1995 Caervallack made their dream come true. It had an old orchard, a listed Well-House, and the vestiges of a garden, with a few mature trees including two medlars. They had come 'looking for a garden' and found it, since, for them a house and garden formed an entity.

Mathew, although a practising architect, has a degree in philosophy, which, as he remarked airily, 'makes me a thinker'. 'The garden,' he continued, 'is a place for spiritual expression' – his wife, echoing his remarks, added that there were within it 'rooms for contemplation' (page 22, top left). She herself had studied art and is a professional painter. As a consequence they are both 'interested in beauty'. Their garden is a shared passion, although they tend to work independently – Mathew providing the structure, and Louise then 'filling in' the spaces.

Before arriving at Caervallack, Mathew was already interested in traditional vernacular architecture, and particularly in the modern use of cob – that is the creation of walls from clay and straw (right). As a proof for the planning authorities of its viability for the building of their studio, he built a specimen cob wall for the orchard, with a serpentine top roofed with scantle tiles from Delabole in North Cornwall, although in a style indigenous to West Cornwall. The Well-House had already been roofed with 'tin', but this was replaced with thatch, and backed with a cob wall which now looks as if it had always been there. On the other side

Caervallack

Gardening in the vernacular

there was constructed a matching thatched summerhouse, which was to form a central feature in a courtyard garden.

Louise was not, however, bypassed in all this industry. The garden was never designed on paper, but came about by 'feeling the way'. There had been a straight path leading down the garden from the house, beginning with a small, square pergola. This Louise extended, but then diverted the original pathway off into various directions, to other parts of the garden. Along the base of the pergola she has planted rounded mounds of box, underplanted with santolina. The pergola (left, top) supports wisteria, *Clematis armandii*, and roses. She admits to an obsession with gardening, and had visited many gardens with her husband. Now she pours over many plant catalogues and gardening books. Her planting schemes are then the result of much considered thought, although, as she explains, the eventual outcome, as in her paintings, arrives suddenly as an inspiration, and is not contrived. Naturally, as an artist she is fascinated by colour, though she does not like harsh contrasts, but is rather traditional, being more concerned with the formal structure of the combination. 'Colour,' she admits, 'is like a limb and a part of me.' Some notable associations were observed, for example black tulips beneath blue camassias (far left, bottom), and pink tulips under a purple elder (left, bottom). These are delicately blended rather than contrasted.

In a revealing discussion in which they both developed their ideas, it became clearer how the gardening held a symbolic meaning for them, not necessarily overt, but subject to personal interpretation. One striking instance is a sculpture of an angel holding a dove (above), by John Aulman, a friend with whom Mathew had studied, standing at the head of a rectangular block of slate from the centre of which water bubbled, forming in itself an object of beauty. Mathew explained

that the sculpture was of yew, the longest surviving of all woods, while the rectangular slate was an old mortuary slab from Treliske Hospital. This combination, of living water issuing from a funereal slab, may thus stimulate thoughts of human mortality. Alongside are two metal throne-like chairs, but when asked for the significance of placing these in this context, to dispel any suspicion of undue solemnity, he replied laughingly, 'simply because they look interesting!'.

Two 'set pieces', as it were, in the garden are notable. The courtyard garden (above), flanked by the pergola on one side, and by thatched cob walls on two other sides, with its attached summerhouse is paved with a pattern of square stones and red brick. This contrasts with four columnar golden yews in the centre, with a jar in the midst. Around the base are planted alchemilla, the 'Lady's mantle', with soft foliage and yellow flowers. Deeper into the garden is a thatched, beehive-shaped pavil-

ion joined to a cob wall with ornamental tiling, in which there is an aperture reminiscent of a 'Gothick' window (top right). This, with a hedge, encloses an inner garden, in the centre of which, at the crossing of two brick paths, is a 'mobile' fountain (above) by Michael Chaikin, representing leaves or petals of a flower, with a bird perched above.

The original garden included an orchard above and behind the house, where are a few native and two cider apples. Here they made a vegetable garden. Since nothing in this garden is without beauty, this has been designed in the shape of a trefoil with walls and pathways of brickwork (left). Overlooking this is a colourful gypsy caravan, much loved of the children who have also been provided with a 'Wendy House'. A small shrub maze near the studio also was planted to amuse them.

Near the steps up to the kitchen garden is inscribed appropriately the words, 'He who plants a garden, plants happiness'.

Hidden amongst the growth in one of the borders, is a beautifully calligraphed slate by local artist Jackie Allan (above), which has three quotations inscribed in a decreasing spiral that perfectly expresses the spiritual atmosphere of this enchanting garden:

> 'God Almighty first planted a garden,
> indeed it is the purest of all pleasures'
> 'One is nearer God's Heart in a garden
> than anywhere else on earth'
> 'There is healing in a garden when one
> longs for peace and pardon'.

Caervallack is open under the National Gardens Scheme, and by appointment.

The garden at East Down Barn is one which owes its existence entirely to the commendable resolution and tenacity of its creators. The dwelling (right) was converted from a derelict barn situated in a narrow, V-shaped valley on the outskirts of Menheniot, erected on a platform cut into the side of the hill, leaving a precipitous slope down into the valley bottom beneath. Although Julian and Valerie Sturdy were able to move into the house in 1991, no plans for the garden had as yet crystallized. In negotiations with the contractor, however, it had been agreed that he would provide a digger to cut terraces in the slope. Nevertheless, on his arrival the driver made it clear that he would need precise instructions, to the inch, as where to cut. Since there was no such precise design, instant decisions had to be taken on an *ad hoc* basis.

By 1992 the ground had in general been laid out, but since the slopes had been found to be full of large stones and shale, they were left virtually barren of soil. Consequently, it was necessary to import loads of topsoil, which had then to be supported by retaining walls. This meant that huge quantities of stone had to be brought in from quarries, and local workmen found who were skilled in the craft of dry-stone walling. All of this involved considerable toil, so that it was some five years before the whole task could be considered completed, during which time it was not possible to carry out any more than sporadic planting on the slopes.

Valerie herself had already gained experience in their own shady garden in Kent, as well as in another which was more open and sunny. She had also taken the opportunity to enlarge her knowledge of horticulture by attending a part-time course in college.

East Down Barn

Gardening a steep slope

With such a background she was able, on coming to Cornwall, to offer her services as a volunteer in the nursery at Lanhydrock, which provided the advantage of a ready source of plants for the creation of the new garden.

By the year 2000 the garden could be said to have arrived at a presentable state, which encouraged Valerie to consider entering for the national 'BBC Gardener of the Year' competition. This involved several stages. At first, photographs were required of the garden which, if they were found

interesting, was then visited. Although still in its early days, it was considered sufficiently developed, particularly since it had been created from scratch, to merit her being selected among a shortlist of six, to design and plant a specimen garden at Harlow Carr. Although she did not win overall, Valerie was first in the 'Garden Knowledge' section of the competition. After the garden was televised, an invitation was received to open under the National Gardens Scheme, something which had not been contemplated.

What, then, of the garden itself? This may conveniently be divided into four quite separate sections – first, the level area around the house, then the terraces down the slope (above), next the valley floor, and finally the stream garden. Originally both sides of the stream had not been part of the site, but Valerie's admiration for the stream garden at Rosemoor led to negotiations with the neighbouring farmer, which resulted in the whole stream being included in the garden.

The wings of the house form a right angle within the arms of which a gravel bed could be constructed. This favourite spot has been filled to overflowing with sprawling geraniums, campanulas, helianthemums, the

Erigeron 'Profusion', and many other low-growing plants. On the terraces along both walls of the house, containers filled with annuals or bulbs have been placed, with hanging baskets on the walls above. Hence, on turning down the steep entrance, one is immediately met by a blaze of colour at all times of the year. The bank along the side of the house similarly has been densely planted, and here, among the varieties to be seen, the now fashionable cerinthe makes an impression, and a spreading *Ceanothus impressus*, with small dark leaves and striking blue flowers, thrives in the poor soil by the side of the house.

A mixed hedge of ornamental shrubs marks the rim of the slope (page 28, left), which faces east, and is thus exposed to the sun most of the day. A gravel path with steps winds down to the valley floor below. The planting here, therefore, is of sun-loving varieties, such as cistuses (top) and halimiums in several forms, notably those with dark blotches on their white, pink or yellow petals, helianthemums, lavender, and hebes oe'r-topped with poppies, penstemons, alliums and foxgloves. A rustic arch on the lower path is covered with roses, wisteria and clematis (above left). Two specimen shrubs of the 'Beauty Bush',

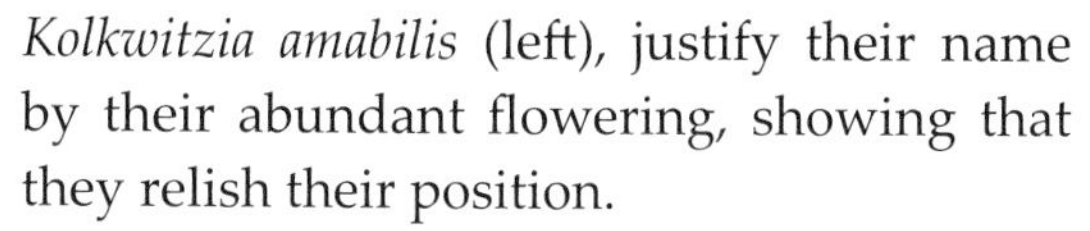

Kolkwitzia amabilis (left), justify their name by their abundant flowering, showing that they relish their position.

The valley floor is more gently sloped and benefits from soil deposited by or excavated from the stream. Here there is space for a lawn with trees – conifers, a tall white leptospermum, a liquidamber and a small *Cercis* 'Forest Beauty', surrounded by several varieties of cornus. One feature of this level is a gravel bed (top). An adjoining bed, once planted with various ornamental grasses, has been replanted since it was felt that the individual varieties tended to lose their attraction after a year or so.

Finally, the acquisition of both sides of the stream opened up the possibility for growing bog plants, such as the beautiful candelabra primulas. A small rustic bridge (above left) crosses the stream, from which these various plants can be viewed.

The creation of the garden at East Down Barn has been a long saga, which says much for the determination of Valerie and Julian, but they are now able, if not to relax, at least to enjoy the fruits of their labour.

The garden is open alternate years under the National Gardens Scheme, and also by request.

Carole Vincent's garden is the realization of an early dream to live in a cottage by the sea with roses round the front door (page 34). As a child she made blocks in her father's building works, and as a student gardened for pocket money. Half Acre stands alone among our selection as the only garden which, as befits an artist, was consciously designed, having been planned on paper and then reproduced as a small-scale model.

Carole came to Boscastle as a teacher in 1961, where she discovered Half Acre which, after renting she was able to buy in 1968. It stood in a field, open to the north-west winds which blew in from the Atlantic coast. Christine Kelway's classic book *Seaside Gardening,* published a year later in 1962, describing her experiences at Trebetherick, a few miles down the coast, was strongly to influence Carole in her choice of plants for the garden. She tells how she sat in an upper room looking out to the cliffs, whose sweeping curves suggested the design for her 'cottage garden'. Her plan with sketches, which is covered in lists of plants for the various beds, still survives (see Carole Vincent's *Concrete Works* for this and her later works). Besides teaching, Carole was painting and sculpting in stone and wood, her penchant for construction being given an outlet when she converted the piggery alongside the house into her first studio.

The 1980s were a time of development and change. First the roof began to leak, which called for renovations, and in 1982 a commission from her former headmistress for the sculpture *Reunion* radically changed the nature of her work. Since bronze or stone would have been too expensive for the sculpture, it was made in concrete, which

Half Acre

An artist and sculptor's garden

awakened a realization of the potential of this material for sculpture. A time of experiment followed, with several commissions, culminating in 1988 with the design for the *Armada Dial* – a huge sundial – in Plymouth city centre, Carole's first major public commission. In the following year she bought the adjoining field, which translated Half Acre into a full acre. The immediate outcome was the satisfaction of her longing, by the building of an ample, well-lit studio (top right), while at the same time affording her an opportunity to extend the garden.

At this stage she had not yet considered anything more advanced than enlarging the existing 'cottage garden', so levels were changed, walls were built and steps cut between the various sections. Much of this still survives. It was now possible to erect a pergola with roses (above), leading to a pool with a sculpture *Twelve Good Men and True* – portraying her parents and friends, and reminiscent of a jury in court (far right, above). Along the side of the pergola is a striking topiary – a plant-sculpture perhaps? – of a reclining cat, *Big Green Bessie* (right). Much of the rest of the garden, however, was later to be superseded.

Up to 1992, Carole's concrete mixtures had included various natural aggregates which, when polished, gave them their colour. A pause, free from commissions, however, encouraged her to experiment further with pigments to produce brilliant, yet stable

colours in concrete. Since these could now survive in the open, the idea of a 'Concrete Garden' evolved, which would demonstrate that 'it is possible to have a colourful environment, not only in the plants, but in the hard landscape'. This was an innovative concept, since traditional hard landscaping is confined to stone or, at its most colourful, to brick. Thus in 1994, with the help of a few students on vacation, a significant portion of the cottage garden was removed, and the 'Concrete Garden' begun. There were to be two ponds, one oval at ground level, the other smaller and circular at a higher level, a spiral with red steps, and perimeter walls originally in blue. Curving concrete brick edging delineated the different ground levels. All was

The woodland, situated across the shared entrance drive from her cottage, is an area for wildlife and flowers. It also contains a 'dead hedge', which was first devised by a friend to withstand the ferocious winds experienced on Alderney in the Channel Islands. Its recipe has never been published and may be of interest to others with similar problems.

surrounded by shrubs and trees, with plants in sculptured pots standing on the walls, arranged around the ponds, or planted in the gravel. Carefully selected places were found for sculptures, such as *Quartet* (above), which is placed behind a sitting area, rendering a silent accompaniment.

In 2000 a visitor suggested that this garden deserved to be shown at Chelsea. After negotiations with a sponsor it became the model (page 33) for The Blue Circle Garden at the 2001 Show, being awarded a bronze medal. Carole has since designed another Show garden, the Concrete Jungle, to demonstrate that 'the simple formality one may expect in the city' may be complemented by naturalistic planting, but although accepted for 2004, it failed to find a sponsor.

The 'hedge' (right) is made of stakes, obtained from the prunings of big trees, inserted in two lines two feet apart, at five-foot intervals. Bamboo canes are driven in between each stake, and bound together and to the stakes with string. The two lines are infilled with twigs and waste too big to compost, optionally with logs at the bottom. Such a construction, a useful receptacle for waste, has been found to withstand the strongest winds, and forms a habitat for wildlife.

Carole sees herself as a true 'Renaissance Woman', combining art with science. As well as cement technology she is interested in maths and construction. 'We have lost,' she regretted, 'the sense of not only designing, but making'. This she has herself most signally done in her sculpture and garden. Half Acre opens as shown in current guides.

Higher Truscott was an old Cornish longhouse, which has been extended over the ages into a small farmhouse. John Mann came here with his wife, Gilly, in 1962. The 'garden' was then no more than a farmyard, with a *shippen* – that is a cowshed – and threshing floor to the side, and a rubbish dump at the end. This site, at an altitude of 550 feet, as marked in the grounds, is windy, suffering from the bitter east winds, which, more than frost, can burn and destroy shrubs and trees, although the greatest losses have come from the effects of damp. The soil was stony, and neutral as a result of some soft rocks of a limey nature, reflected in the presence of nearby limekilns, so that special soil had to be prepared for the growth of acid-loving plants. Altogether, then, the site presented a challenge to a prospective gardener.

The garden was created by John, a busy vet based in Launceston, as he admitted, 'as an escape from work', although for many years it had to compete with family, dogs, ponies and visitors. A conservatory was erected at the back of the house, with a view over beds of low-growing plants (right), across a lawn on to the trees at the far end, which include conifers, *Magnolia wilsonii* and a large 'Handkerchief Tree' (*Davidia involucrata*). But before this was built, what was dubbed a 'sit-outery' – a sheltered place to sit in the sun – was created (page 40, top) to give a cross-view to a sunken rose-garden, now with a circular trough of alpines (page 40).

The clearance of the farmyard and the improvement of the soil progressed but slowly. The object has been 'to maintain the vernacular' by the use of local materials, especially granite, and country objects

Higher Truscott

A hardy plantsman's garden

such as stone troughs. John's first love was for herbaceous plants, but it soon became apparent that these were simply blown over by the force of the winds, so that the range of planting had to be extended to shrubs and trees to afford the necessary protection. Although his 'bible' was Arnold-Forster's classic *Shrubs for the Milder Counties*, none of the tender or experimental varieties described in the book could possibly be grown in these harsh conditions. But Arnold-Forster had himself experience of a wind-blown garden at Eagle's Nest, on a rocky pinnacle open to the sea near St Ives. Even so Launceston, and Truscott, are about as far from the sea as anywhere in Cornwall.

An interest in rhododendrons (right) was aroused by John's acquaintance with A.M. Williams at the nearby Werrington, which had been a repository for rhododendrons collected during the expeditions of Forrest. Albert Williams, on visiting Truscott, remarked on the labelling of the plants, since so many of the labels for Forrest's introductions at Werrington had been lost or confused during a period of neglect during the Second World War. From here was received a layered plant of 'May Day', a hybrid raised at Werrington. Another of John's mentors was

Rene Moffat, the revered gardener at Penheale – a fine though relatively unknown garden with contributions from Lutyens and Jekyll – with whom John had many conversations, and from whom he received plants.

It has been the intention to create year-round interest in the garden. To this end, the hellebores have become somewhat of a speciality. The well-known 'Christmas Rose', *Hellebore niger*, a species that requires a more alkaline soil, did not thrive here. Other varieties, however, were to prove more successful. They were first introduced in the leafy soil under the trees at the end of the garden where they flourished. These were supplemented by a friend who stopped over at Truscott *en route* to his holiday, who 'paid' for his stay by bringing hellebores. These, which were mostly of the purple variety, were 'left to the bees' to propagate, which they did profusely. This encouraged the introduction of several other species, which were then manually fertilized to produce a whole range of beautiful seedlings which were distributed throughout the garden, where they would flourish under shrubs like philadelphus and deutzia, which were pruned back in the winter, and in combination with ferns and perennials that favoured the same conditions. A striking group, seen from the conservatory and grown with daffodils, contrasts with the bark of an *Acer griseum* (above). Although these seedlings have remained unnamed, a hosta, which has self-propagated, has been named 'Truscott Marble', and has been taken up in commerce, although it seems probable that it will be renamed. This interest in woodland plants has extended to fritillaries,

and to epimediums, of which there are now thirty-six varieties growing in the garden.

Another unlikely enthusiasm to be pursued in this inhospitable environment has been alpines, notoriously difficult in Cornwall. However, these have been successfully grown in troughs filled with grit to the brim (page 40). The plants, from the roots of which the soil or any peat has been removed, which would induce the growth of moss, are planted in pockets of grit with a little seed compost an inch below. As the photographs demonstrate, this has proved remarkably effective. A small alpine house is now devoted to a display of lewisias.

In 1980, the daughters and ponies having departed, the paddock across the lane became available for cultivation. Here wide, sweeping island beds have been created, planted with an array of perennials, shrubs and ornamental trees for year-round colour (see clematis, above left). Through the trees in the hedges are distant views of Launceston, and of Dartmoor beyond. At the far end a neat vegetable garden has been laid out (above), with cut hedges leading to a summerhouse, between which herbs are grown.

Higher Truscott is a striking example of an initially unpromising site being tamed enough to satisfy a desire to cultivate a wide range of plants. John Mann has been a chairman of the Cornwall branch of the Hardy Plant Society, and is now President of the Cornwall Garden Society.

The garden is open one Sunday each in May and June.

Ince Castle, an early seventeenth-century house of a rare type, although built on an ancient site, and ripe with legends, had never had any reputation as a garden until the arrival in 1960 of Viscount Boyd and his wife Patricia, who created the whole garden on what was virtually a virgin site. 'Ince' derives from a Cornish word meaning 'a promontory', which exactly describes the spot, set between two creeks on the Lynher river.

The estate is at some distance from the main road, and is approached along a straight drive, embroidered on each side in early summer with cow parsley intermixed with orchids and other wild flowers, arriving at the entrance pillars surmounted with lions brought from Wivelscombe by the present Lady Boyd, where the west front opens on to a carriage ring and shaven lawns, uninterrupted except by the overhang of an ancient Turkey oak.

The formal gardens extend from the south side in a regular sequence, beginning with a paved terrace, which has recently been reduced in size, rich with crevice plants of which the most conspicuous is the rampant *Erigeron karvinskyanus*. A lead tank, dated 1752, stands in the centre with a *putto* fountain (page 46). The terrace leads on to a lawn with flowerbeds along the walls, built each side as a protection against wind. The lawn is without plants except for two free-standing wisterias. A few steps lead down to the Sundial Garden (right) which is quartered, with each bed planted with a mixed array of shrubs and herbaceous plants. The obelisks, which are now enveloped by foliage in summer, have been superseded by four *Magnolia stellata* as accents. The sequence is completed by the Lily Garden, with a narrow pond or

Ince Castle

Gardening around an historic house

canal longwise across the width, leading the eye to an hexagonal Shell House (above). Among the lilies and irises two intriguing *putti* ride on snails (above right). On returning, the Castle is seen through the thickly planted beds of the Sundial Garden, or above a varied foreground of lawn and terrace.

If the path behind the Shell House is followed through the trees, it arrives at the walled Summer Garden which Lady Patricia chose to set up in isolation, and where she grew the more colourful plants, among them a collection of salvias which has now been increased to sixty varieties. The space beyond the Lily Pond is occupied by the swimming pool (page 47), from which there are panoramic views of the Lynher and the countryside beyond. The pool, with semicircular ends, has an obelisk at each of the four corners, echoing those in the Sundial Garden.

To the west, between the drive and the wall of the formal garden, lies the tennis court and white garden. A path along the side of the court, passing an intriguing wrought iron seat outlining a cat, made by artist

Richard Bawden (above), had originally led to the Kitchen Garden, which also included Lady Patricia's stock plants for sale on open days. This has now been reshaped into two walks, with mixed shrub and herbaceous borders on each side (above right). Lady Patricia continued in command of her garden almost until the end of her life in 2001 – her husband had died in 1983 – but her son and daughter-in-law, the present Lady Boyd, moved from the neighbouring Wivelscombe to the Castle in 1994, amicably sharing the responsibilities.

It was the Lawn on the east side of the house which was Lady Alice's' immediate concern until the death of her mother-in-law. Here the parkland opens out on to a most spectacular vista over the Ha-ha to the waters of the Hamoaze and Plymouth beyond. The earth from the levelling of the lawn has been used to raise the Mount from the top of which an even more commanding view of the city can be seen.

At the south end of this side of the house Lady Patricia had formed along the wall a parterre, known from its shape as the Castle Garden. The four quarters of this garden have each been planted with red and white thrift, camomile and thyme. More recently a hornbeam hedge has been added around the garden, but looking south past the white bench seat a glimpse of the Lynher can be discerned through the shrubs. The centre of the house is used as a sitting out area

shaded by an awning. The iron staircase, which leads up to the first and main floor of the house, is draped in summer with racemes of wisteria (far left). At the northern end a conservatory with a small forecourt was added in 1995, which is used for tender plants and climbers. Again, through the windows and flowers the view of the city over the water still dominates. A cherry walk from the conservatory leads into the woodland.

The larger trees in this woodland are all that remains at Ince of the original 'garden'. It has now been underplanted with rhododendrons, camellias and other woodland species (top). In the centre a glade, known from its shape as the Oval, has been cut out. At the west end is the Water Garden where a stream trickles over rocks thick with ferns and other woodsy plants. Looking from here across the grass, full of wild flowers in early summer, a vista opens up through the trees to the waters of the Tamar and Hamoaze.

Little space has been available to write about the planting at Ince, a deficiency which it is hoped is remedied by the photographs. It may, however, also be objected that a garden of this type is out of place in a book of this nature. Its justification is that the garden has been due entirely to the devotion of Patricia Lady Boyd who created it out of nothing, taking full advantage of the unique features of the site, where the various compartments flow naturally into each other. It is a remarkable example of a post-war garden, unique in Cornwall, which can stand comparison with any in the country.

Ince Castle Garden is open on one Sunday each in March, April, May and July.

Ken-Caro, where Kenneth and Caroline Willcock came after their marriage in 1966, was one of the earliest among our selection to have received notice in a national survey of open gardens in 1987, although in fact it had been open under an old Gardeners' Benevolent Scheme (now part of the National Gardens Scheme) since 1970. It was at that time a much smaller garden than it is at present, arranged around a bungalow sheltered by high hedges. This garden still survives, although the Willcocks have abandoned the bungalow in favour of a larger dwelling higher up, which has reproduced a feature of the former design by having a rockery running along the rising ground by the side of the house. The name 'Ken-Caro' has an authentic Cornish ring (*kehn* = ridge; *carow* = stag) for a site on the brow of a hill, near a former deer park, but evidently it is derived from the two Christian names.

In 1992, and again in 2002 the garden was extended to a total of about four and a half acres, on bare ground at an altitude of some 450 feet, sloping towards the north-east, with spectacular panoramic views over Bicton Woods to the hills beyond (right). The soil is very acid and the rainfall high, although this drains freely down the slope. When I first saw this garden, the extensions were protected with artificial screens along the ridge, and it seemed inconceivable that any plants could survive in such an exposed position. Now, when it flourishes apparently without such protection, I was told that the shelter was indeed still there, but in the form of shrubs.

Kenneth has a long experience in horticulture, having cultivated his own garden as a child in a home where his father and

Ken-Caro

A connoisseur's garden

grandfather had been commercial vegetable growers. From such a background he had acquired the skill not only to plant hedges and screens to filter the wind away from the more tender plants, but also to select those which could stand up to the prevailing conditions. Among these are various hollies, and a collection of griselinias, some from Ireland, such as the variety 'Bantry Bay' which is no longer obtainable there. Phormiums, which are not averse to wind, became a speciality as much for their all-year colour and form as for their wind-hardiness.

The object of the planting has been to provide colour through the season. Ken-Caro's hydrangeas (above) have become renowned for their intense blue, generated by the very acid soil, which in late autumn develops into a dark purple. This colour is intensified by the close association with the blowzy white panicles of the *paniculata* varieties.

Visitors in the summer have been heard to remark on the apparent shortage of camellias, but there is a fine collection distributed throughout the garden, including 'Joan Trehane' and 'Grand Jury', names which betray their origins in New Zealand, from which many of the varieties planted have been imported. There is also a collection of magnolias, which has merited recording in a recently published survey of magnolias in Cornwall. The newly introduced yellow varieties of *denudata* (far left) do particularly well and flower later than most. Acacias also thrive in the open, two varieties of *A. baileyana purpurea* (left) being grown which respond well to being pruned, and thus may be expected to shoot again if cut by frost.

The season is extended by the use of herbaceous plants. Very few annuals are grown, although dahlias have again come into their own, and now exhibit a number of varieties

with coloured foliage. All of these, as well as other plants are widely distributed throughout the garden in large beds, some protected by evergreen hedges or sturdier plants along winding paths on the higher ground. Other long beds curve through the lawns, leading the eye to the view beyond, the picture often being completed by billowing white clouds against a blue sky. Two lakes have been dug, the planting around the higher one coming into maturity, that in the lower part of the garden (above) being more recent.

So far the planting in the garden has been described in general terms. The commonly used expression 'plant association' seems to have no precise meaning, but tends to vary considerably in practice. Consequently at Ken-Caro it will be seen in its own distinctive form. Kenneth himself became skilled in flower arranging, and this may be reflected in, or perhaps has grown out of, the associations of the plants in his garden, although he does not himself make any such connection. Nevertheless, unlike those who may enthuse over the colour schemes of their herbaceous borders, not a few commentators on the garden here have pointed to the combination of just two or three plants. Kenneth himself will remark on the beauty or effectiveness of some particular grouping – it may be a purple magnolia against a background of yellow daisies; or of a pink dahlia alongside a tree of *Acacia baileyana purpurea*; or the startling red stems of a rheum in front of the cod's roe flowers of a dwarf *Trachycarpus fortunei* (right). These perhaps seem unexpectedly sensitive insights in one who describes himself as 'a rugged country sort of person'. Nonetheless, they are a characteristic of the garden which will become the more apparent the more it is looked for, since the attribution of this as 'a connoisseur's garden' was that of visitors, and not of Kenneth himself.

In conclusion, although I have not so far mentioned the name of Caroline, Kenneth

would be the first to remind us that she has been at all times his collaborator in the creation of this garden, so that is was with a sense of tragedy that she recently suffered a stroke. Happily she has recovered sufficiently to be able to descend from her mechanical wheelchair still to play her part in the garden.

Ken-Caro has welcomed visitors from the outset, and is still open from late February until September, except on Saturdays.

Kingberry had probably once been a farm, but was for many years a market garden and orchard. As the town of Bodmin expanded to envelop the outskirts it became a private dwelling, which it had been for some forty years when Matthew Stead, who has a medical practice, and his wife Harriet, also a physician, moved here in 1991. Thus, unlike many of the gardens in our selection, it had the benefit of long cultivation, with a neutral soil in good shape.

The urban sprawl had resulted in the house being entered unpropitiously between two garages into a confined area flanked by a high wall leading to the entrance door at the side of the house. But all this was not long to be left unadorned. The area was soon paved and invitingly planted with hostas, sedums, billowing grasses and pot plants to welcome the visitor (page 58, top). A golden yew stands to the left of the entrance, while to the right a gate under a tall brick arch tempts one to enter up steps to the back of the house. Here was once a narrowing strip of waste, which might understandably have been left neglected. Instead, an attractive small garden has been created here, which would be a model for those limited to cultivating a backyard. A small formal gravelled area leads on to a long paved path, which runs to the end of the house where the borders overflow on to the pavement. The wall from the entrance archway, draped with honeysuckle, is sloped to meet a smaller arch nearer the house.

From the archway, across the entrance door is seen the alley through which the garden proper is approached. This unappealing defile between the end of the house and a wall is relieved by an ancient pear tree climbing the wall of the house, which bears

Kingberry

A town garden

small sweet fruit in its season, by ivy overhanging the opposite wall, and by a hanging basket (left), so that when viewed from either end it arouses an anticipation that there is yet more to come, as indeed there is.

The treatment of these problematic areas at the entrance to the grounds illustrates the ingenuity with which Harriet has shown herself able, as it would appear almost effortlessly, to transform what otherwise would have been a gloomy passageway into a thing of beauty, a facility which is evident in the garden itself.

The house, which is on a slope, had no view, except of the roofs of the buildings around, so that the object has been 'to draw the eye inwards'. This was achieved principally by retaining the old wall of the orchard and raising hedges whose dark foliage not

only excludes the surrounding dwellings, but acts as a backcloth to the colourful borders in front of them (above). Harriet's interest has been confined almost entirely to herbaceous plants, disposed through the various sections of the garden as incidents, rather than as formal borders. She was, like many others, inspired by the associations of colour at Bosvigo, but has interpreted them in her own way. There are, for instance, no brash contrasts such as she may have admired in Christopher Lloyd's garden, but had no intention of copying.

The garden and principal front of the house open on to a rectangular lawn with borders at each end and a plain hedge on the long side. There is an ample terrace along the front of the house, providing room for the planting of close-clipped bushes in the shape of globes and two pyramidal pittosporums on each side of the door, interspersed with low shrubs such as fuchsia and mahonia. The global motif has been repeated on the edge of the terrace, although here alternated with low plants in pots. This planting is designed to lead the eye past the 'hot' border on the lawn, out into the farther side garden.

Here a conservatory has been built along the side of the house, to be used rather as a sun-lounge than as a plant house, which opens a view through to the end of the side garden, bounded by three ornamental trees – the white *Cornus kousa chinensis*, the yellow-foliaged *Robinia pseudoacacia* 'Frisia', and the silver 'Weeping Pear', *Pyrus salicifolia*. Along the old wall of the orchard to the right, a wide herbaceous border has been planted with blue and purple flowers

in various shades towards the conservatory (above), with lighter colours towards the white cornus, where there is a doorway into the old orchard. Even here the ancient trees have not been left without the adornment of two rambling roses.

Along the left side of this garden the hedge runs without a border, and in a central alcove stands a plinth with a striking sculptured head by a member of the Shona tribe, brought from Zimbabwe (page 56). This hedge appears to be entire, so that it comes as a surprise that at the end an arch leads into an unexpected 'secret' garden. This enters on to a platform with a white bench seat, where the shed is covered by a 'Kiwi Fruit' *Actinidia chinensis*, from which can be viewed an expanse of foliage plants, dominated in the centre by a young *Catalpa bignonioides purpurea*. The whole effect of this innovative garden has been achieved by the planting of varieties with striking foliage in a range of subtle colours, where flowers are incidental, such as rodgersias, hostas, phormiums, grasses and rushes (above right). Along one side is a small pool (right), destined to be embellished with a fountain and a sculpture. In contrast, a brilliant blue pot stands at the end of the central gravel path (far right).

Harriet is perhaps too unassuming when describing her garden, where the variety of the design is so satisfying, and the modulated colour schemes so delicate. It was therefore not surprising that she chose the tranquil foliage garden, a place for quiet contemplation, as her favourite.

Kingberry is open once or twice a year for charity on no fixed dates.

Lamorran House is favourably situated in a road winding down past the Castle along the coast to St Mawes which, with its little white houses and harbour, is reminiscent of the Riviera. Robert Dudley-Cooke, who had a holiday home nearby, was immediately struck by Lamorran's closeness to the sea and the possibilities for laying out a garden on the undulating, south-facing hillside, with the continued possibility of yachting (which, however, was soon to be overtaken by an enthusiasm for the creation of a new garden).

Forthwith, his collection of plants from his home in West Surrey, where he had specialized in azaleas and rhododendrons, being chairman of the Wessex RHS Rhododendron Group, was moved by container to Cornwall, where indeed many had originated. Here he planted a collection of some 500 evergreen azaleas (page 64, left, with rhododendrons), almost all of which he had propagated himself, with the aim of producing continuous flowering from early spring until June and July, by planting the *indica*, and 'Satsuki' varieties, which he had researched, receiving a generous gift of rooted cuttings from the Plant Introduction Center in the USA. He was an avid reader of gardening books, including those by Michael Haworth-Booth, whose 'close-boskage' style of planting he was to emulate. (See also page 128.)

The Dudley-Cookes took up weekend residence in 1982, and began to create what is surely today a most astonishing example of 'weekend' gardening. The family would travel down by rail on a Friday night from London, from the law practice which Robert had founded as a young man and, with the help of his wife, Maria-Antonietta, he

Lamorran House Gardens

A Mediterranean garden

devoted twelve hours on Saturday, and ten on Sunday, to creating the garden, before catching the train back to the city again. Their small daughters meanwhile were able to play while the work proceeded.

Once the tangle in a neglected garden overgrown with thickets had been cleared, it was the Japanese style which initially was to influence the design – a pond with a waterfall being the first to be constructed in the centre of the garden, to be followed later by a koi pond near the entrance drive (right). From here the ground sloped steeply down to the rear of the gardens of the coastal cottages below. The first task was to clear the ground and cut out winding paths and steps. A watercourse was constructed to feed into a sequence of pools. Although facing a little east of south, to avoid the full blast of the south-westerlies, and shielded by the high ground above from the north, some protection was essential, and it was decided that this was to be achieved, not by a perimeter belt, but by planting shelter trees strategically throughout the garden.

As the planting developed, exploiting the mild marine climate by selecting tender varieties such as the acacias, eucalypts, cordylines and trachycarpus, the garden began to take on a more Mediterranean air, which accorded well with St Mawes itself. Various Italianate features, such as statues, urns, a well and a rotunda were introduced, all discreetly placed where they might appear surprisingly at a turn of a path, or be seen on the heights above, even though they may have looked a little stark before the trees and shrubs had grown around them. It was now the famous Hanbury garden at La Mortola, and later the garden of Lady Walton in Ischia, which became the predominant influence, reflecting Maria-Antonietta's Italian connections. It is significant that although the influence of the Tresco Abbey Garden is pervasive in Cornwall, it is never mentioned here, since, although similarly exotic, the design of the Abbey Garden is on quite different lines, with straight parallel paths intersected at right angles.

As the garden began to mature, the opportunity arose to extend the grounds

by adding a further two acres at the bottom, which was undertaken in two stages. The first section was planted with palms and succulents in the open, not all of which were at first successful. Reflection upon the conditions in the now flourishing upper garden made it clear that it was the Australian plants which were better able to stand the dampness of the Cornish winters, rather than those from New Zealand, where the winters are drier. The succulents similarly benefited from a light canopy of leaves rather than being in full exposure.

The soil is a light, acid sand, in most parts over shale, which is very free draining. It required considerable improvement, even to the extent of importing quantities of woodland soil from elsewhere. During the course of clearance numerous granite rocks were uncovered, which after repositioning through the garden helped to create a rockery where such exotics as aloes, aeoniums and agaves could nestle below their protection and be given sharp drainage (right). By these various expedients it has been found possible to grow a wider range of plants in less favoured situations: for instance thirty-four different varieties of palms now flourish at Lamorran (see 'Palms' in *Gardening on the Edge*), which help to create the feeling of a garden on the Riviera, enhanced by the many vistas over the blue waters of the bay to the headland beyond. In the 1990s it was suggested by the

RHS that some of their students might gain experience in this unusual garden, which led one of them to apply for the post of head gardener, a position which at that time did not exist. After due consideration, he was appointed in 1994, and has remained ever since. However, much of his time now the garden is mature is taken up with pruning back the extensive growth, which is unfortunately the inevitable consequence of the 'close-boskage' style of planting.

The garden at Lamorran House remains a private garden, to which the owner is deeply committed. Nevertheless, visitors will be welcome generally on Wednesdays and Fridays, from April to September.

Landewednack House is the former rectory of the southernmost parish in the British Isles, a little over a mile from the Lizard Point. Marion and her husband Peter Stanley moved here in 1994, to a garden no more than a quarter finished after a residence of only two years by their predecessors. Much lay unfinished, and there were heaps of rubble and granite blocks around the grounds.

The garden of two acres, though near the coast, is in a dip and sheltered from the wind. There had not been a frost in ten years until 2003, ironically at a time of panic about the increase of global warming! The soil is a neutral loam, dry from a low rainfall except for 'sea fret', or mists, which quickly clears.

Marion had been trained as a biogeographer, which involved the study of botany, a subject which had interested her from her childhood in the countryside of Worcestershire. Later she gained experience in market gardening and the growing of vegetables in Derbyshire, where chrysanthemums were a speciality, receiving the wise advice from an old gardener that 'you have got to put the heart back into the soil'. Before coming to Cornwall she had already created three gardens, the first in 1976 on limestone. In the meantime she had studied art, which gave her, as she explained, 'a strong sense of the juxtaposition of colours', which may be said to have reached its maturity in this present garden.

In discussion it became clear that every stage of garden-building had been carefully thought out, and could be described in every detail. This is apparent to a visitor even on entering, where you are immediately confronted by a 'Tresco-esque' bed which includes palms, agaves, aloes,

Landewednack House

A colourist's garden

aeoniums, fatsias, castor oil plants, melianthus, echiums, and more (above). It was undoubtedly intended to make an opening statement that this was to be no usual garden. On a more practical level, however, it owed its origin to the need to relieve the starkness of the blank gable wall of the house.

Marion is not a lover of orange, but an exception was made in the entrance beds (far right), where she considered bright colours welcoming. French marigolds, an orange-flowered pelargonium, and an orange grass were characteristically contrasted with dark foliage, and the *Fuchsia* 'Thalia'.

The entrance to the house (right), simply laid out to lawn, has a flagstone path leading to the front door, bordered with dwarf box cut into the shape of globes, which pessimists had warned, wrongly as it turned out, would not survive the salt winds. Along the edge of the lawn to the garden front of the house is planted a narrow 'braided' bed of annuals – ageratum, lobelia, white busy lizzies (the more vivid colours were avoided) in place of alyssum which did not flourish. Here the object has been to provide continuous colour throughout the summer at a conspicuous point of entry where the cars are parked. This bed is aligned with the church tower, which is an eye-catcher in its own right, as well as being relevant to the garden's origin.

The vista over meadows past the church and along the coastline is not visible from the general garden level, so that a pathway

has been cut behind the shrubs on the bank opposite the entrance door, which leads to a gazebo with a high enough view to look beyond the garden, and provide a 'hide' to watch the birds which, unconscious of any presence, hop, sing, and build nests.

On turning the corner to the garden front one's eye is immediately caught by a vibrant herbaceous border (page 72) along what is discovered to be an unusual wall built of the unique indigenous Lizard serpentine. Marion is insistent in describing this bed as a 'cacophony of colour'. Beds of graduated colours as she had seen at Hadspen are difficult to achieve, as well as being contrary to her own instinct to create incidental groupings of colours, some blended, some complimentary,

and others contrasted, which, although individually harmonizing, in their overall effect in a long bed might be deemed cacophonous. These combinations are highly personal, created by the choice of carefully selected, and often unusual varieties, which shun the conventional or fashionable. The 'heart' has been put back into this bed, as long ago advised, by dint of the heavy digging in of farm manure and spent mushroom compost, and by regular mulching.

Alongside this border, by the house, is a herb parterre. The far side of the lawn has been built up from granite blocks found around the grounds with two flights of granite steps descending to the garden below. This retaining wall is edged with a long bed of lavender accompanied by a 'froth' of the delicate pink rose 'Ballerina' (page 69). Roses are a speciality, of which eighty-three varieties are grown, the dreaded blackspot, endemic in Cornwall, being controlled by regular spraying of the plants and soil from January onwards. Marion describes this lower area as a 'busy' garden, where grass paths weave between beds of varying sizes and shapes, each with its own character – an old cherry tree forms the centre of a white garden, another pursues the sub-tropical theme with 'King Proteas', leucodendrons, echiums both single and bushy, and cannas. A 'hot' garden around a pool with water lilies lies in a hollow overlooked by a summerhouse – designed by Marion herself with stained glass in the windows – beside the swimming pool above.

There had always been a vegetable garden here, which now also grows cutting flowers – dahlias, and old-fashioned, scented sweet peas in soft purples and pinks. The latest additions are posts with swags of rope supporting perpetual ramblers and *viticella* clematis (right). One side is bordered with blue agapanthus and marigolds.

In 2004 it was decided to transfer to a more manageable property, so one sympathizes with Marion's sorrow and regret at leaving this highly individual and personal garden. Its future is uncertain, except that it will inevitably express another's personality.

To attempt to create a garden on this site cannot be described as anything but heroic: it is a prime example of gardening against the odds. Before turning, then, to the garden itself, something must be said about the conditions out of which it sprang.

Par in the seventeenth century was no more than a tidal creek, used by Daphne du Maurier as the location for her novel *The House on the Strand*. Waste flowing down from the inland copper mines gradually silted up the creek to form marshes, allowing the building here of a small, thatched cottage. By 1870 the mines had closed, and the pumping of water from the adits ceased, so that flooding began again when the land water met high tides from the sea. One solution seemed to be to build up the level with infill, obtained from wherever it might be: stones, clinker, domestic rubbish – anything but soil. The cottage was enlarged into a 'Villa' in the 1930s, but flooding continued every winter. In 1970, however, the Water Board began a water release scheme, creating a Defended Flood Plain, passing through the garden, where the marsh is separated from the cultivated part by a watercourse, which can be controlled by sluice gates, and this has proved successful.

All this was ancient history when in 1985 Judith, from Leicestershire, with her husband Harvey Stephens moved down from a farm on Bodmin Moor to his family home, where she decided to create a garden. Nevertheless, what may have been ancient history was to become a present problem. Cultivation was to begin in the yard, which consisted of hardcore. There was nothing for it but to engage a mechanical digger to turn it over and break it up, and dispose of the

Marsh Villa Garden

A damp garden

rubbish. But soil had to be brought in – from any passing lorry carrying soil, from road sweepings and leaves, silt from the marsh, and loads of farm manure, compost and imported topsoil. Now, in early summer, a bed on a filled-in trench in the yard has a border of vibrant purple and blue herbaceous plants and tulips (above).

A deep culvert from the flood protection scheme left an area of built-up ground which, it was decided, should be lowered to form a sunken garden, entered down granite steps retrieved from a disused barn. At first the idea was to enclose this in a yew hedge, but this proved unsuccessful, so clipped privet has been used instead (above right). Judith had no plan for the garden, and had little opportunity in a working life to visit those of other people, but she gained her knowledge from reading, evidently with some success in the selection of trees, which were her first enthusiasm.

She had been allocated a strip in a three-acre field, shared with the house-cow from which it was separated by a barbed wire fence. Here she was determined to grow something fast and tall, for the whole site was barren of trees, except for two old apple trees. She at first planted isolated willows, poplars, alder and eucalypts. This meant excavating holes with a pickaxe and iron rod to clear out the rubbish, before bringing in decent soil for planting. Very slowly beds were formed around the trees, and eventually joined up to make walks. Many ornamental trees could now be added to the foundation trees – catalpas, two paulownias, a fine 'Swamp Cypress', davidias, several birches,

and a liriodendron, although this list does not by any means exhaust the great range of ornamental trees now in the garden.

The demise of the house-cow released the remainder of the field, which now seemed just the place for a pond (pages 78–9). Ironically, although the garden was once a marsh, and part still is, digging down to the first water level was not successful, since it dried out in summer. Expert advice was sought, which recommended that nothing short of digging down twelve feet to the water table would suffice. This left a cavity like a quarry, but it worked. The surface of the water in summer is now about six feet below the surrounding ground, and a path dug around the pond is flooded in winter when the water table rises.

There had been much underplanting along the walks, but Judith began to long

for real herbaceous borders. A square was now selected and surrounded by an escallonia hedge, originally conceived as a wild garden, but having been convinced of its impracticability, it became the formal herbaceous garden. Although it was at some distance from the house, a similar hedged garden at Lanhydrock seemed to be justification for this position. This now has three borders, two along the hedges, and the third as an island bed. That on the right is a 'hot' border (page 77, bottom), with a pink, blue and purple border on the opposite side. The central bed grows the taller plants. The preparation of these beds was no easier than elsewhere. Again a mechanical digger

needed to be brought in to loosen the hard ground, which then had to be worked over by Judith and Harvey to clear large stones, lumps of china clay, old bottles and clinker – probably from the Par gasworks – before any attempt could be made to improve the soil. Judith, who describes herself as strong and healthy, has always loved heavy farm work. Without such sturdy qualities none of this garden could ever have been created.

Beyond is the marsh, lying lower than the garden, and reached over a channel of water with a sluice at each end. In the dry season the marsh appears to be woodland with streams running through, and is technically known as 'willow and alder carr', but in winter it can be flooded. It is a protected wildlife area (left).

Judith concluded her account of the garden with good advice to anyone hardy enough to attempt a similarly arduous task – 'No matter what you've got,' she said, 'something will grow!'

Marsh Villa Garden is open Sundays to Wednesdays from April to October.

The garden at Nansawsan House is alone in this series in having an underlying historical structure. It is, therefore, fortunate that Michael and Maureen Cole, who came here in 1975, should have an interest in history, which in this case is many-sided. The original house was built in the mid 1870s by the rector of Ladock for his curate. Stamford Raffles Flint, who came to occupy this position, was a man with an interesting lineage. He was the great-nephew of Sir Thomas Stamford Raffles, Governor of Sumatra, who established the settlement at Singapore, and a great-grandson of Major-General William Mudge, who carried out the first of the ordnance surveys, of which that of Cornwall, published in 1813, was the earliest. Flint himself became rector of Ladock, and was later a Canon of Truro and an Archdeacon, although he remained at Nansawsan, while the former rector, his cousin, continued at the rectory. In the 1890s he enlarged the house in two stages to accommodate his growing family. His daughter Alison, who had a rhododendron named after her, married George Johnstone of Trewithen, an expert and writer on magnolias.

After Flint's death the house and garden had a chequered career – empty from 1925 to 1940, in military occupation during the Second World War, and the house and garden split into three parts in the 1950s. The present Nansawsan House (page 82) consists of the original section, with a significant part of the garden. The large lawn below the raised terrace in front of the house, open to the countryside beyond (page 83), was probably part of the original landscaping at the time of the building. It was in the areas between this lawn and the main road where ornamental planting had been carried out.

Nansawsan House

Restoring a Victorian garden

When the Coles arrived, they found that the garden had not been radically changed through its many vicissitudes. The main garden had been well maintained by their predecessors, who had also planted a productive fruit garden. However, during the years the house was unoccupied a thick belt of cherry and Portuguese laurel, and *ponticum* rhododendrons had become well established, as is typical in Victorian gardens. All of this would require heavy clearance if, as they intended, any new planting was to be done.

One of the earliest areas of clearance arose out of a recommendation from a former gardener of Lord Falmouth at Tregothnan, who had been engaged to prune the magnolias. After looking around, he suggested that a plot along the boundary would make a good side-garden. This is now known as 'Mr Ough's garden'. The previous owners had already re-erected a chalet brought from the seaside town of Perranporth, which was typical of such buildings in the 1930s. Although a great deal of restoration was required, the front retains its original appearance to form a feature at the end of this 'Bluebell' garden, named after the chalet (top). A path which snakes its way through the lawns, planted with daffodils, was restored and other paths were made following the Victorian desire for curves. Much later, in the mid-1990s, a greenhouse in a Victorian style was added at the other end of the lawn (above). This area was covered with clinker, probably from a

wartime field kitchen, although after rejuvenation it grew strawberries splendidly. Two beds, one of evergreen azaleas, the other of the deciduous variety, were dug in the lawn.

The practice of naming sections of the garden, principally as a means of identification, has continued. During one of the clearances a pump emerged. Upon investigation a ringed slab was discovered which, on being raised, uncovered a bricked chamber which evidently had been constructed to hold rainwater. Once this had been cleaned out, the pump could be restored for its original purpose, rather than as an ornament. The 'Pump Garden' (page 84, top right) is now planted with hybrid and *yakushimanum* rhododendrons.

'Victoria's Garden' was named after a statue of a Victorian child uncovered during the cutting back. Unfortunately this was later stolen. One of the most recent additions, a round gazebo with a pointed roof, which can be seen from the entrance drive above a bank of red evergreen azaleas (pages 80–81), is sited to look down into this garden.

In the border along this side of the main lawn there are mature tree heaths, which flower in the spring and early summer, when their purple contrasts with the yellow of daffodils. Rising above is an immense yew, which has been colonised by a wisteria, whose racemes drape the branches to the very top. In the summer this is a remarkable sight from the raised terrace (page 84).

Although these various gardens have been formed out of relicts of the original garden, they are not intended as reproductions. The policy has been rather to preserve the atmosphere of a Victorian garden. In this

respect Michael's enthusiasm for the older varieties of rhododendrons has been able to contribute to this effect. In the first place he has collected several of the early Cornish hybrids now forgotten, if not actually lost. There is a cream hybrid from Penjerrick; another, 'Sir Charles Lemon', commemorates the celebrated owner of Carclew, and Chairman of the Royal Horticultural Society of Cornwall; and the 'Duke of Cornwall', one of the Gill hybrids from Tremough (now the campus of the Combined Universities in Cornwall), which won a prize in the Cornwall Garden Society Spring Show in 2004. Another of Michael's interests has been in the old Ghent deciduous azaleas (right), similar to the orange-flowered *calendulaceum*. These beautiful, soft-coloured azaleas have undeservedly been displaced by the more vivid colours of the modern hybrids.

Although this was not the Coles' immediate intention, the potentiality of an acid soil, and the resulting concentration upon ericaceous plants has made Nansawsan a more typically 'Cornish' garden than most of the others in this book. But it is rather as an illustration of a sensitive restoration of a Victorian garden that it has merited inclusion.

The garden at Nansawsan House is open in April and May under the National Gardens Scheme.

Peterdale is the smallest of the gardens in this book, a mere third of an acre around a modern bungalow lying unprepossessingly on the outskirts of Millbrook, near the Cornish border. Ann Mountfield, formerly a hairdresser in Leeds, moved here in 1979 with no knowledge or experience in gardening, to a garden overgrown with weeds and brambles on stiff clay. Her first contact with plants was in a local flower-arranging group, where she was attracted by the foliage and flowers brought by the arrangers, many from their own gardens. Members encouraged her to take home cuttings of the plants she fancied, which rooted surprisingly easily. This awoke a fascination for gardening, which resulted in Peterdale becoming one of the most extraordinary gardens in the country, winning the RHS Silver Bowl for the Best Family Garden in 1995.

Ann began by avidly reading library books about gardening, which wisely guided her first steps, to root out the weed, including the dreaded couch grass, and dig in loads of farm manure which she wheeled over from the adjoining fields. The climate is mild, with infrequent frost, and little troubled by winds, being in the lee of a hill. A stream drains the water from above. In only two years she had the garden ready to open to visitors locally, and a year or two later was invited to join the National Gardens Scheme. Perhaps more to the point, during a visit by the President of the Floral Art group she was complimented on having 'a gift for plant association', which I well recollect confirmed my own impression on my first visit in 1985. For many, this would be praise enough to relax and bask in approval. But Ann had, to use a colloquialism, 'been bitten by the gardening bug'.

Peterdale

A small Feng Shui and Japanese garden

Not satisfied, she began to redesign her garden because, as she said, 'it looked like everyone else's'. She had become inspired by the books of Margery Fish, although she found her garden woefully neglected when she visited it. Nevertheless, she sensed her presence everywhere. Many features of this second stage remain – in front of the house, instead of the familiar drab privet, she had planted *Berberis darwinii*, the red *Cotinus*, the double-flowered gorse, the juniper 'Pfittzeriana Aurea', and other evergreens. Along a bank at the side she created a rockery with rocks from a local quarry brought back in the boot of her car. But her experiments led her in the direction of the Japanese style, which, as had become her custom, she studied indefatigably, even visiting the Chelsea Flower Show for ideas.

The rear garden slopes upward, and it was decided that the new Japanese garden should be created at the top. An essential Teahouse was constructed (above left) in which tea was laid out in the traditional manner. On the right, an open pergola was erected (above right), with an upper floor which gave a panoramic view of the garden and neighbouring fields, on the Japanese principle that one should 'borrow the landscape'. Below, Ann herself dug out a pond, which is crossed by

a bowed bridge (far left). The general planting is in character – the 'Heavenly Bamboo' (*Nandina domestica*), two acers, 'Satsuki' and *japonica* 'Vitifolium' colouring red in the autumn, an *Acacia dealbata* with yellow flowers, and the giant-leaved gunnera. The scene can be contemplated from an arbour covered by an Albertine rose.

Ann had observed all plants to need careful positioning, 'as with a compass', and had become convinced that the arrangements should have meaning. These ideas she discovered were reflected in the Feng Shui philosophy. Thus, in 1993 she resolved to design a Feng Shui garden opening from the patio doors of her living room, to represent the eight 'Enrichment Methods', which are: (1) Friendship and New Beginnings (at the entrance); (2) Relationships; (3) Children and Family; (4) Healing and Peace; (5) Wisdom and Experience; (6) Wealth; (7) Fame, and (8) Pleasure and Indulgence. It was left to the individual how this might be interpreted in their own designs.

The garden is square with white walls, although pierced with 'windows' (page 90) and a door out into the middle section of the garden, while along the house there is a pergola with a vine. The exotic planting is in raised beds on the walls, the most

striking feature being a central circular bench seat, painted blue, at which a group might sit and converse. In the middle is a smaller ringed bed decorated with a bright mosaic (far right), which might be a recollection of the coloured tiles that Ann had seen in the garden of an Italian in Leeds as a child. It is not possible here to describe the whole design in detail, but it is significant that she has chosen a birdbath, for the seven doves who visit her garden, to represent 'Wealth', just as it was agreeable to know that the table and chairs where we were entertained to tea represented 'Pleasure and Indulgence'.

Between the Feng Shui garden and the Japanese garden, although a central Tibetan Cherry forms a link, was Ann's last experiment – a Mediterranean garden. This might be described as minimalist, since the ground is wholly covered with yellow gravel, with only the occasional aloe, agave or other spikey plant rising through (top right). The cast metal table and chairs here are again painted blue. It is indeed a well-sheltered area, which on a sunny day with reflected heat, and a coloured umbrella overhead, creates an illusion of being on a beach in the Riviera.

This is a garden full of imagination, atmosphere, and ingenuity, which reflects the personality of its creator. Unfortunately, Ann's means did not permit her to remain in this appealing garden, although it is hoped that it has passed into sympathetic hands. She has now moved to one in a group of retirement houses, where she misses her garden greatly, although one suspects that she will soon have ideas for a new design on a much smaller scale.

Pine Lodge has, almost certainly, the finest collection of plants – over 6,000 varieties – in the South West. It is ironic, therefore, that a garden visited internationally by groups from botanic gardens should have been created not by a botanist but by an enthusiastic gardener.

Ray and Shirley Clemo came to Pine Lodge – named after the trees which once surrounded it – in 1974, without ever dreaming of creating the varied gardens over such a wide area that it has now become, and which at that time they would have felt to be overwhelming. As with many a garden, it all began by planting around the bungalow, and it was at this stage that Shirley, trained as a photographer, became fascinated by plants. By the 1980s a quite sizable garden had grown up around the house. The main entrance passes through light woodland, later replanted on one side with an underlay of camellias, while the other side, carpeted with bluebells and bulbs, was relieved by occasional shrubs, ending in a Secret Garden. The earthen path was laid out as a serpentine walk in brick, which arrives at a Koi Pond, fed from a waterfall, where a sculptured puma (right) prowls beneath an *Acacia pravissima*. The front of the bungalow is now reached over an arched bridge (page 94).

The garden front is terraced in red brick with four *putti*, representing the seasons, standing on the front wall, in the centre of which is a small cascade emanating from a frog's mouth. In the front lawn is a wide, circular sunken garden with a fountain in the centre (page 95), which affords a home for smaller plants and alpines. The grass paths from this point wander on through large mixed beds containing a variety of trees, shrubs and herbaceous plants which had

Pine Lodge Gardens

A world of plants

caught Shirley's eye. One corner of this area is still described as the 'Cottage Garden'.

By this time the variety of unusual plants was already beginning to catch the attention of specialist groups – I myself first visited in 1985 with a conservation society – and was otherwise open only occasionally for charity. The style of planting, later to be found throughout the garden, was developing. The plants were selected principally because they were of interest, and were arranged not systematically as botanical specimens – although there is a National Collection of grevilleas – nor even by their country of origin, but where it was thought they looked best. Growing contacts with botanic gardens, and trips abroad, enlarged the repertoire of plants, seed catalogues from as far away as Japan being read alongside gardening books to widen the number of varieties selected. Most of the new introductions were brought back or sent as seeds, and were then propagated at home.

Shirley's early childhood training had taught her to be meticulous, which is illustrated not only by her determination in keeping the garden weed-free, but in listing the plants. They are all named, labelled, and researched as authentic before planting, then recorded and increasingly photographed in leaf and flower. It has surprised some that such a large estate – it is some thirty acres – should be included in a book on 'hands-on' gardeners, but those who have watched Pine Lodge developing will confirm that for many years Shirley has herself laboured from dawn to dusk, to be taken out on Saturdays by her husband to prevent her from working!

As the garden grew Ray Clemo, who modestly claims the garden to be entirely the work of his wife, became an ally. First he gave her statues as Christmas gifts, and then went on himself to collect and restore many intriguing artifacts in the garden: cast iron seat ends, bollards, and above all granite – features, slabs, and sets reclaimed from abandoned railway stations and other sources. The first granite steps led down into the Arboretum of mixed deciduous trees and

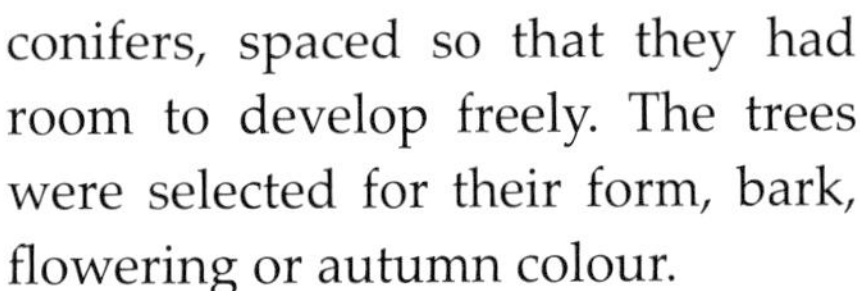

conifers, spaced so that they had room to develop freely. The trees were selected for their form, bark, flowering or autumn colour.

The Water Garden was dug out and planted with a hedge of hardy-hybrid rhododendrons, at first to ward off a threatened incursion from the adjoining highway. There is now an impressive stand of the massive-leaved gunnera along one side, water lilies on the surface and lilies, iris and other water plants along the fringe. The Slave Garden was created to join the water gardens to the main garden with a paved walk, the low hedges being punctuated by narrow conifers. Here Shirley surrounded the Slave with a selection of grasses (above). The perimeter of this central area is edged with three herbaceous beds, which are individually colour-themed predominantly in blue, yellow and red hues. The surrounding lawn has been planted with fourteen different varieties of magnolia.

At the far end of the main garden, the Arboretum has been extended on the right into a Pinetum (above right), where the eighty conifers have been arranged so as eventually to form an amphitheatre, the trees increasing in height to the rear, although with the varied rates of growth this will take some years to materialize. The field to the left has been treated as parkland, gently sloping down to a lake, adorned with black swans.

The most recent project was inspired by a visit to Japan, where it was recognized that one of the gardens seen would fit conveniently into an area of the grounds which had till then been left waste. One of the deciding factors was that the existing background of mature trees matched those in the Japanese garden (right).

Today, advancing years and the need to consider the future when they have no descendants to succeed them, has resulted in the garden being opened regularly to the public. This has led to the provision of a car-park, a refreshment area and a nursery. Nevertheless, a visitor may well be welcomed or shown around by Ray himself, and will see Shirley at work in the garden, which they still regard as very personal to themselves.

Mark and Claire Woodbine came in 1982 to the Pinsla Lodge on the by then unused drive to the Glynn estate, which was overgrown with *ponticum* rhododendrons and roamed by wild life – badgers and feral deer from the old deer parks in the Cardinham woods. Mark, from near St Austell, had experience in his grandfather's garden, but Claire, from London, where she had worked backstage in the theatre, knew of nothing but a small town garden. 'Gardening,' she now declares, 'is definitely an art form' and opportunity for self-expression, although generously admitting that in their case it is a combination – Mark who is practical and the labourer, while she is pragmatic and experimental. It is this bewitching aura of the wild woodland infused into this special relationship that has shaped this most unusual garden.

After clearing the ground the first step was to begin a vegetable garden. Although as 'a follower of fashion' Claire was instinctively 'organic', Mark applied his experience in gardening to digging compost and 'Growmore' fertilizer into the poor shaley soil, and learning how to control pests: self-sufficiency required productive crops. In those days there was no time to spare after putting the house in order and building an extension, so that the 'garden' was lawned over, with a few flowers, but was decidedly rough.

Horticulture and garden design were to be learnt, not from books or lectures, but on the ground from practical experience. The admitted influences surprisingly were not those usually mentioned by other gardeners in this book, but such as Gertrude Jekyll at Hestercombe for her 'plantscape', Rosemary Verey at Barnsley, Monet and other French gardens, especially the 'Peace' garden in

Pinsla Garden

A romantic garden

Paris. But these were inspirational rather than models to follow slavishly. How then was this all to turn out?

Both Mark and Claire rejected, if not despised gardening by rule, and what they described as colouring by numbers. The rainfall here is extreme, some 55 inches a year. Although not a frost-pocket, the winters are too cold for tender plants, so that the garden has grown by stages, experimenting to find the plants which would thrive in these conditions, and by trying out various combinations that they found pleasing. The intention was not to create conventional herbaceous borders, but to associate plants together in a naturalistic way and as a haven for wildlife. This eventually led to wide beds of mixed herbaceous and shrubby plants, but not neglecting annuals where they would be appropriate. The ground would be worked over in October, when early-flowering plants, such as violas, which might have been swamped or had rotted could be replaced, and the associations between plants could be reviewed and if necessary changed until they 'worked'. The beds – for there are now no lawns – were separated by paths cobbled with patterned slabs intended to complement the plantings (left), which could in this way be viewed from differing angles. Near the house the raised beds are planted with lower varieties and alpines, with ornamentals

such as agaves in pots, and later hanging baskets, for 'the garden is meant to be an extension of the living space'.

The overall objective therefore has been to work towards finding a design which, as they said, 'would be right for here', in classic terms to discover 'the genius of the place', an objective which they feel to be nearly but not yet quite achieved.

So far our account has been of an intensely personal garden described in conventional terms. But Mark and Claire's quest has led them in directions which the unsympathetic might dismiss as eccentric, although it is exactly these aspects of the garden that display the greatest creativity. The more cultivated part of the garden merges gradually into the surrounding woodland, where paths have been mown through the swathes of wild flowers. In that air of mystery which can so often be sensed in the wild woods, one here begins to notice unusual features. At one's feet, as if creeping through the grass, is a red serpent or dragon consisting of flowerpots! One bay of the uncut grass ends in a ring of stones, 'magic' perhaps? Beyond is a primitive stone circle, and in the distance a 'pagoda'. Near the boundary, metallic strips hang from a small tree, over a shape formed from interlaced twigs (above left).

Such so-called 'eccentricities' are not confined to the woodland. By a gate stands an

arrangement of bare tree trunks and oak roots (page 101, right). Near the house a shelter has been constructed by Mark, with rugged pillars of white stone discovered when digging the soil (left). Many of the iron fences have been extended into bizarre ornamental forms. What does all this mean?

Actually on enquiry there are often reasonable and quite unromatic explanations – a surplus of flowerpots, stones left over from digging a cesspit – but in essence these are works of the imagination, which emerged almost unconsciously during their disposal. Their meaning is inexpressible. When I cautiously suggested that it would not surprise me if I were to see wood nymphs appear through the trees, I was delighted to hear Claire agree, by replying 'Definitely!' It is for these reasons that this can be described as a 'romantic' garden, defined more solemnly as 'the culture of romantic spaces to alter people's perception of reality'. Their acid test is, 'Does it work?'. It will be for you to decide.

Pinsla has been open since 2001 when it was accompanied by a nursery, which replaced the vegetable garden. It is conceived as integral to the garden, and arranged like a parterre. There are many unusual plants on sale, but just as the garden is an amalgam of the artistic and common sense, there are no lack of familiar names. It is open daily from March to October, and then at weekends.

The house at Readymoney Cove stands facing the sea, just across the road from the shore. It had once been the stables for Point Neptune, the Italianate marine villa built by the second William Rashleigh of Menabilly in the 1860s. From 1942 to 1943, as a tablet reads, it had been the residence of Daphne du Maurier, where she wrote *Hungry Hill* before moving up to Menabilly – the origin of the name 'Manderley' for the house in her novel *Rebecca*.

Stephen and Margaret Read moved here on their marriage in 1957. As with Daphne herself, they used the garden during these early years to grow vegetables, and as a playground for their children. Serious gardening did not begin until their retirement in 1992, when their family had grown up and moved away.

The front of the house as seen from the road has the appearance of a neat cottage garden, with roses, clematis and passion flowers climbing up the walls, and a winding path edged with blue aquilegias leading to hydangeas by the house. In a trough by the gate, seasonable flowers are planted in spring and summer, and a line of 'Naked Ladies' (*Amaryllis belladonna*) springs up along the outside wall in the autumn. But all this belies the quality of the garden behind.

On the western side of the house, a stream flows to the sea offering the opportunity for the creation of a bog garden. Small plants such as the drum-head primulas, dwarf daffodils and the white endymion, grow alongside the stream (page 106), while yellow candelabra primulas contrast with ferns and the purple-leaved rodgersia. Later, light yellow grasses intermingle with groups of deep blue irises (page 107). Along this same path one comes surprisingly upon a specimen

Readymoney Cove

A seaside valley garden

collection of bricks made in fifteen different Cornish brick works during the period 1832 to 1910, which is an indication that this is a garden which will exhibit a wide range of interests.

A conservatory has been built on the rear of the house, which opens on to a sitting area for *al fresco* meals, enclosed by fencing with a variety of ornamental plants, among them a fine *Clematis florida* var. *sieboldiana*, and a container with a large *Fuchsia* 'Thalia'. This enclosed area leads out on to a croquet lawn, a game which is taken seriously by the Reads, who are members of the Cornwall Croquet Club. Along one valley side there is a greenhouse and a summerhouse. At the far end, a fine early-flowering magnolia, possibly *Magnolia denudata*, spreads its wide branches over a carpet of primulas, which when in full flower are a magnificent sight. Indeed, as Margaret rightly observed, although this is intended as a garden for all seasons, it is perhaps at its most colourful in the spring.

Beyond this lawn is a now unused hard tennis court, although this is sufficiently hidden not to obtrude on to the garden at large. It is redeemed, however, at the end where the ground has been planted with part of a collection of some twenty-five species of bamboos introduced by Stephen, who at one time had been a member of the Bamboo Society.

The main garden lies on the floor of a narrow valley in a frost pocket requiring protection for the less hardy varieties in the winter. The opening section has been

laid out in colourful formal beds, with winding gravel paths leading to an Arbour (page 105). As a curiosity on the side, Daphne du Maurier's bath, retrieved from the house, is preserved as a receptacle for evergreen azaleas and other pot plants (page 107).

The stream which runs along the valley bottom, edged with water plants, refreshes a luxuriant sward in which have been cut out various themed beds – one with hostas, another with ornamental grasses, and yet another area given over to the naturalized southern marsh orchid, which is hybridizing with an introduced similar species from Madeira. Orchids are one of Stephen's special interests, which he pursues in the small heated greenhouse packed with exotic species, with towards three hundred varieties. In this he has benefited from his son, who, as a biologist working in Ecuador, has supplied him with many seeds of unusual varieties.

Two slates have been arranged to encourage nests of slow-worms, the intriguing legless lizard welcomed by gardeners as a predator of slugs. They complement the four-legged newts that breed in the ponds. Throughout the garden are interesting stones and driftwood thrown up on the shore; one striking example resembling a horse's head is given pride of place on a pedestal (above).

The south-west side of the valley – the north-east side being part of another estate – is able to sustain a few ericaceous plants which cannot be grown in the slightly alkaline soil below. This is also the place for the vegetable garden, which boasts a line of genuine Victorian clay rhubarb forcers, with lids at the top for the foliage to emerge in its own time. Following a traditional coastal agricultural tradition, countless barrow-loads of seaweed are hauled up from the beach every year as fertilizer.

Two recent features have been created on the higher levels. The first, by Margaret, is a shell grotto made from shells collected by hand from the beach. They are artistically arranged as flowers in blue tile pots, which are matched by surrounding actual pots planted with blue flowers. In a niche, as in a shrine, is a statue of Hsi Wang Mu, the Chinese goddess of the Western Hills (above), but intended as an object of beauty, rather than for worship!

Farther up the hillside walk a viewing area has been created, with seats made of timber grown on site and floored with flat stones from the beach, which gives a panoramic view over the cove to the estuary of the Fowey river beyond (right).

The garden at Readymoney is a treasure trove – a testimony to the far-ranging interests of the owners. It can be visited principally during the Du Maurier Festival in May.

Thomas Tonkin, the eighteenth century Cornish historian, wrote that, 'the desire of our ancesters [was] to settle in our vallies, and to get, as they call it in *the luthe*', that is 'in the shelter'. There could be no better description of Rose Cottage, one of three which nestle down in a hollow below the road, sheltered from the cold north winds.

Paddy Powell, the daughter of an Irish doctor, was born in Bodmin where he practised. Although she worked 'up-country' her heart remained in Cornwall, so that in 1976 she bought Rose Cottage as a weekend retreat, retiring there with her husband in 1983, a ruined seventeenth-century house below being restored as his study. Later, when a lower cottage became vacant, they were joined by her sister. When they had settled permanently, the verge of the road above the lawn became available. One of the men working on the cottage at the time was recommended as an expert in the craft of dry-stone walling, known in Cornwall as 'hedging'. Thus Gerald Duke came to be engaged first to wall the verge, and then to help in his spare time with the construction of walls and paths in the garden. He proved himself to be an artist and this happy association lasted for many years until, at the turn of the century, he became too ill to continue.

After her husband's death in 1991, Paddy began to link the three cottage gardens into one ornamental whole, and serious planting now began. The lower cottages are approached by a lane, but at the top a gate and entrance opens into the garden of Rose Cottage itself, with a path leading down steps on to the front lawn. The planting here was to become the focal point of the garden. A fine urn on a pedestal was placed to the left

Rose Cottage

A moorland cottage garden

of the steps (left), which could be seen from the central window of the sitting room of the cottage. Above the steps, on acid soil, were planted a *Rhododendron yakushimanum* and azaleas, a *Magnolia stellata*, camellias and hydrangeas, which now flourish on each side of the entrance path.

The bank, formerly the road verge (above), which runs to the left of the urn, has a shillet soil which was planned as a silver and grey border, but has been infiltrated by gold, as in the flowers of the fine euphorbia by the urn. Among the silver-grey varieties are perovskia, the herbaceous and shrubby senecio now known as brachyglottis, santolina and argyranthemums.

A second and more convenient entrance opens from lower down the side lane around the opposite side of the lawn. Here is a wide bed planted in a cottage garden style, with a medley of colourful flowers, although with a rather more sophisticated choice of varieties (page 114). Paddy is particularly fond of oriental poppies, of which there are many varieties here and in other beds. They are joined by alliums and lupins, as well as roses, one of which has a curious history.

In 1979, while working for the BBC, Paddy travelled to Castle Howard to interview the notable garden designer James Russell, who presented her with a pot which had arrived from East Germany that very day. It contained the rose 'Irene Watts' which, he said, had been lost to cultivation in England. This now flourishes in this border with a fulsome flower almost like a peony.

Growing in the beds along the front of the cottage beneath a window is a handsome clump of zantedeschias (above right), while a rich blue clematis, 'Perle d'Azur', climbs up beside another, contrasting with wine-coloured hollyhocks. To one side in a corner, water gushes into two basins from the mouth of a fantastic bronze sculpture of a fish (left).

Ultimately the gardens to all the cottages came under Paddy's care, at first with the help of her sister, and then, after her death, in her own hands. The lane is now edged on one side with trimmed globes of box (above, far right), intermingled with a variegated ivy, which is lit up in summer by the brash orange of the common montbretia in the hedge above. A low wall runs from the lower entrance to Rose Cottage around the paved courtyard of the next cottage, which has been

planted with bright alpines, matched by the various pots that adorn the forecourt.

The lane now passes down to the lower garden where there is an arbour with a seat from which the meconopsis around a pool may be contemplated, or a countryside scene of meadows won from the moors can be viewed. A *Magnolia grandiflora* grows against the mullioned windows of the old house, and a pergola on the gable end, covered with wisteria, looks down a sloping triangular lawn. The lane narrows to a path through beds planted with shrubs and perennials, among which apricot and white foxgloves mingle with hostas. A *Magnolia sieboldii* has been strategically planted on a bank, where its hanging cups may be viewed from beneath. On the far side of the lawn the stream has been reshaped into a cascade, so that the air is filled with the sound of plashing water.

For Paddy, the garden is full of the memories of her husband and sister, and reminiscences of its laying out with the help of Gerald Duke. The charm of this garden lies in its preservation of the exuberant feel of the cottage style, while concealing the skill and artistry that has gone into the planting, so that it all appears to be quite natural.

For several years Rose Cottage was open once each year for a 'Garden Day', but it attracted such a large number of visitors that it was adopted by the National Gardens Scheme to make it more widely known, although not thereby losing the festive air of a village event. The time of opening will be found in the NGS 'Yellow Book'.

St Martin's is not a manor, but a former rectory alongside its parish church. It is a fine Georgian house, with a sloping drive past tall trees underplanted with ferns to reveal a lawn surrounded by grand Turkey oaks and beech. Ken Olson retired here in 1988, as much because the land would give him a free hand to create a garden, as liking the house. He had come from Sweden to practise as a surgeon in London, living at first in Brompton Square. On moving to Wilton Crescent, which had no garden, he bought a weekend cottage near Henley, where he inherited an old-fashioned garden and gardener. When the opportunity arose to employ his own gardener, the garden was redesigned in a formal style with terraces, where the planting was 'very polite and sophisticated' in soft colours, which was to become quite celebrated locally when it was opened.

The move to Cornwall, of which he had little experience, was made when he was looking for somewhere larger to retire with a friend. There was no garden here – the 'lawn' was no more than rough grass, and there were, to his surprise, no plants at all – in other words, the typical garden of an uninterested cleric. The grass is now a lawn with a handsome urn as a focal point at the end, and the house is surrounded with foundation beds and climbers. On a stone terrace stands a simple and functional wood table with chairs, for Ken abhors fancy garden furniture and ornaments.

The main door is at the side, facing a bank clad with a variety of shrubs, which continue to the rear – and it is here, around a corner, that one is startled to enter a new world – an exotic paradise. One of the editors of *The Good Garden Guide*, on see-

St Martin's Manor

Gardening with hardy exotics

ing the garden, declared that he 'considered it the best summer garden he had seen in Cornwall'. But how did this come about?

The house took two years to put in order. During this time Ken would lean over the hedge of the paddock to the rear and dream of his new garden. The field sloped south, levelling at the bottom; the soil was sand over shale, free-draining, sheltered from cold winds and protected from frost – altogether a favoured site for a garden. The field, which had been grazed by sheep, was dug over with loads of farmyard manure so that it has required little feeding since, except for the application of compost. Ken had decided that there certainly must be a pond, for he loved 'the wonderful lush vegetation around ponds', although at this time he had no idea how lush it would become (pages 116–17). Once the laying out of the garden began, steps up to the higher level were constructed, at first of railway sleepers, which were soon found to be too slippery and so were replaced by those of stone. This was obtained locally, since it was felt that a mixture of materials in gardens is out of place and 'bitty', so that nothing is allowed here but local stone and gravel.

At this early stage the garden was formal, and 'politely' planted as at Henley. But on one occasion a nurseryman friend brought a gift of cannas, a plant Ken despised in corporation park borders. They were nonethe-

less planted discreetly, in case his friend came again. But when he saw their coloured foliage and elegant form as they matured, they began to go up in his estimation. This experience was followed by a visit to the sub-tropical garden at Overbecks near Salcombe in Devon, which was a revelation and changed his whole idea of gardening. He now sought out other plants with striking or large foliage. Soft colour gave place to the strong colourings of the sub-tropical plants. The pond began to be surrounded with large and exotic foliage – banana, gunnera, bamboo and cyathea, a delicately foliaged tree fern. An unusual Australian 'Black Boy' was also planted in this area (page 118, left). The adjoining beds were planted with many coloured cannas, and agapanthus. Later a rill with a small waterfall flowing into the pond was added (page 119). There was no plan, varieties were planted where they seemed to fit, and sometimes the natural growth of the plants would produce surprising and unexpected effects.

Some visitors have described this manner of planting as masculine, creating 'a man's garden', by which they probably mean that it is in contrast to the more delicate shading and contrived associations seen in feminine gardens. The effect of the large and varied foliage is indeed bolder and the strong colours more dramatic. The planting of the pond could be interpreted as 'a theatrical setting',

perhaps for a jungle, a term Ken sometimes uses himself for his garden. The pond garden is undoubtedly unique, and essentially expresses his own personality, where he will sometimes walk in the twilight with a glass of wine, luxuriating in the lush foliage and scents, which he describes, with some hesitancy at using such a word, as 'magical'.

The garden on the slopes above is more conventional (above). There are long island beds in the middle section, through which steps lead to a circular paved terrace, with a bed of succulents – agaves, aloes and yuccas above the top wall. Over the steps at one side hang the faintly obscene reddish flowers of the *Beschorneria*. Along one bed Ken is attempting, for his own amusement, to form a border graded in rainbow colours, a difficult task not yet achieved. This is but one example of his attitude towards gardening, which is one of enjoyment. Although he protests that he is not a garden designer, and knows nothing about plants, he has an eye for a good variety and will exult in the elegance of a form, or the shape of a leaf, or the exquisiteness of a flower.

St Martin's Manor is occasionally open for charities, but more usually on request.

Trist House is named after an unusual succession of grandfather, father and son as incumbents of Veryan on the Roseland peninsula. Jeremiah, the father, had built himself a separate mansion, but in 1835, after his death, his son Samuel exchanged his living in Devon to take over the old 1720 vicarage, which he rebuilt, probably to the designs of Henry Harrison, a London architect then working in Cornwall.

It is ironic that Brenda Salmon and her husband should have come to this old vicarage in 1994 from a rectory in Sussex, which they had run as a college, where she had already created a large garden. From her proximity she had learnt much from visiting Sissinghurst, and a reading of Margery Fish's *We Made a Garden* led to a pilgrimage to East Lambrook, where they became great friends. She learnt from these gardeners what she describes as blowzy planting kept strictly under control.

The initial attraction of Trist House was that it was a 'blank canvas' within a framework mostly of evergreen oaks. Brenda had no clear design in mind when making her preliminary survey of the grounds, but found no signs in front of the house of any previous garden, other than what were known as the 'Italian Terraces' below the west front (page 124). Since these are not aligned with the centre of the present façade, it seems likely that they date from the earlier 1720 house. They are too narrow for any elaborate planting, but lead down to grassland, probably originally grazed by sheep. It was here that the reshaping of the garden was to begin.

The grass was first levelled as a croquet lawn, with a summerhouse and swimming pool to the north, screened by a flower-bed. Along the west side a long rainbow-coloured

Trist House

Rediscovering a Georgian parsonage garden

herbaceous border was thickly planted. Below this a cherry walk was underplanted with blue hydrangeas. Brenda's intention at this stage was to reproduce the style of her planting in Sussex by creating a predominantly herbaceous and rose garden – as she described it, a 'jewel' in a Cornish setting. Her knowledge of shrubs and trees was as yet, she admits, decidedly elementary.

Brenda's objectives in designing the garden are most succinctly stated in her own words in an article she contributed to the journal of the Cornwall Garden Society – 'we decided to create a semi-formal garden to echo the formality of the house, with different areas leading through the garden, defined and distinguished by colour, shape, style, and levels rather than by walls and hedges.' The first of these levels was the long straight 'Dining Room Walk' running north from the house (above right), later planted with magnolias to the rear. This straightness was disapproved of by a visiting garden designer, but was retained resolutely for its value as a vista from the dining room. One of her characteristics has been to form 'long beds of continuous planting'. Here there is an edging of *Narcissus* 'Cheerfulness' in the spring, and *Schizostylis* 'Viscountess Bynge' in the autumn. Further terraces below, echoing the 'Italian Terraces', were added later.

Roses were to be one of the major features in the garden – some two hundred varieties being grown. To this end a pergola 150

feet long to support a 'Rose Walk' was constructed along the terrace and conservatory at the north side of the house (left). Many varieties of climbing and other roses were chosen for their recurrent or continuous blooming. Roses are notoriously difficult in Cornwall, but Brenda found that by growing them on their own roots, and feeding them two or three times in the year they will flourish. The pervasive 'black spot' is attacked by heavy pruning in July and August. 'Albertine', for example (page 126, left), when cut back to the main stem, sprouts and flowers again quite quickly. A rill was dug alongside the pergola, although artificially pumped since there is no water in the garden, which is on stony, fast-draining soil.

But what of the old garden? It was deduced that the Pleasure Grounds must originally have risen above the house to the east, where a rose arch led to a Folly, possibly constructed from the remains of an earlier vicarage which burnt down in 1683. The woodland includes two huge Irish yews, and a massive 'Cornish Red' rhododendron, above thickets of laurel. This area has yet to be retrieved.

The most astonishing discovery, however, gradually exposed over several years, was a massive and extensive rockery. Samuel Trist, who had spent £3,000 on rebuilding the house, had expended a staggering £1,000 on the garden, probably mostly in conveying great blocks of quartz-veined granite from the close-by Carne quarries near Nare Head. These were piled 30 feet high against stone walling to create the effect of alpine peaks overlooking a lake (above right). By chance,

during research, Brenda came across an illustration from the *Villa Gardener* of 1838, printed in Miles Hadfield's *History of British Gardening* (plate xxiv) of the rockery at Hoole House in Cheshire, which bore an uncanny resemblance to that at Veryan. It seems probable that Trist may have seen and been influenced by this design. The rockwork, however, was found not to end here, but extended through walks to the rear, one of which is planted with bulbs, heathers and azaleas as the Dell Garden. The whole area had been covered by brambles, a huge fallen tree, and four self-sown sycamores, all of which had to be removed before any planting could be undertaken. As well as introduced varieties, this area is rich with primroses, bluebells, foxgloves and other wild flowers.

Finally, mention must be made of the vegetable garden to the south of the house, which had been plagued, as was most of the garden, by rabbits. Rather than leaving it protected with random and untidy netting, Brenda decided that it should be enclosed within palings, and planted formally, which has created a most unusual, if not unique feature (left).

Trist House is open on Sundays and Tuesdays from April to September, and by arrangement.

Those who can do, while those who can't write – to adapt a familiar gibe. I imagine I am not alone when reading or watching media gardeners in wondering what their own gardens are like. Now that I am on my fourth gardening book, the publisher has been kind enough to allow me to write a postscript on my own garden – not to claim that I am a 'creative', but to prove I am not an armchair gardener.

Although always interested in gardening, I was, as it were, thrown in at the deep end by being presented to a living where my predecessor had a reputation as a gardener, and his widow had carried off all their choicest plants. Being 'a poor parson from a town', I spent the first winter deciding which were the best replacement plants within our means, when I came across Michael Haworth-Booth's *Effective Flowering Shrubs*, which became my 'bible'. Large areas of my acre garden were grown in with creeping buttercup and ground ivy, immovable with a fork. I took his advice, turned the clods over with a spade, and mulched up to nine inches deep in leaves, twigs and garden litter. Come spring, the only weeds which could struggle their way through, I could pull out between a finger and thumb – magic!

The next lesson was 'close-boskage planting' – positioning shrubs to meet, in order to suppress weed. It was also suggested, if the soil conditions were right, to plant a majority of evergreens, so that the garden retained its interest in the winter. We are still following all this advice in our smaller garden, regularly spreading our own compost with handfuls of fish, blood and bone.

After leaving my country parish we lived in a London flat for seventeen years, and

Tresillian

The author's garden

chose a small, split-level house on a steep slope as a prospective retirement home. One of the attractions was that the back garden (40 ft x 40 ft) had already been 'landscaped' into terraces. We were to learn later to our cost that, although indeed professionally designed, it had been implemented by a 'Giles family', where everyone from grandma to little Willy took a hand. The terracing had been achieved by filling in the slope with the topsoil, leaving the stony subsoil on the surface!

Nonetheless, since I did not retire for another ten years there was ample time to improve the soil, by dint of digging and the welcome arrival of glyphosate to eradicate the 'Lesser (though greater menacing) Bindweed' in our front garden (20 ft x 40 ft). During this time we bought plants to cover the ground, instead of ice-creams on

holidays, but they had to look after themselves. When our friends occupied our holiday-house, we asked no more than that they cut the grass. Some permanent trees and shrubs were introduced, and here I made my first mistake. The house faces slightly east of south. However, it did not occur to me when planting trees along the lower boundary that eventually they would cast a shadow, making this a north-facing garden. Thus, when we took up residence in 1983 they were cut down, although even lower shrubs still present a problem.

I wanted one or two columnar trees as accents, the first choice being an 'Incense Cedar', which appeared slender in the east of England, but in the west spreads itself – so that came down as well. Nevertheless a *Cupressus sempervirens* 'Swaine's Gold' has retained its pencil-like figure up to 18 feet, and its foliage contrasts well with a nearby *Berberis thunbergii* 'Helmon Pillar' which needs trimming as it gets older, while *Juniperus communis* 'Compressa' is a reliable dwarf. Following the 'great man's' advice we planted shrubs – a 'special' *Magnolia denudata* 'Wada's Form', sundry camellias, rhododendrons, azaleas and hydrangeas, all intended to give a continuance of colour. I made a search for late-flowering evergreen azaleas such as *indica* and 'Satsuki', as well as the lesser-known 'Ferndown' hybrids, and the *Rhododendron nakaharae*, discovering an un-named azalea which flowered in July. Curiously, the small-leaved evergreen azaleas, and rhododendrons such as *impeditum*, never flourished as well as the *kaempferi* varieties and larger-leaved rhododendrons. Neither can we grow gaultherias or vacciniums, or even the summer heathers, except for *vagans*, presumably because our pH is not low enough.

Now, twenty years later, my enthusiasm for 'close-boskage' needs to be qualified,

since 'close' in time became 'smothered', so that painful decisions have to be made as to which shrubs to keep, and which to give to friends with larger gardens. This radically alters the nature of the garden – from a wide variety of growing plants, to a much smaller number of mature but select shrubs.

Like so many Cornish gardeners, my desire to attempt a 'little Tresco' aroused an interest in succulents – aeoniums, agaves and aloes, as well as yuccas, palms and bromeliads. All of these needed winter protection, so had to be grown in pots, suggesting that in winter their place could be taken by daffodils, which could then be 'lost' when their leaves became disagreeable. The ultimate in pottery was to produce a collection of standard camellias and fuchsias, which lifted the flowering to a new level. These are placed in their due season on the outer edges of the over-wide steps down from the top to middle terraces (above). The dull grey of the concrete steps has been relieved by encouraging ornamental ivies to grow along the risers.

Yet age eventually begins to take its toll. Our once admired little lawn, a martyr to winter moss, is now paved, the hedges grown too tall to trim safely have given way to 'hit and miss' fences, where the planks alternate this side or that, which become threaded with the large-leaved variegated ivies and the more rampant clematis, such as *montana* and the evergreen *armandii.*

The ambition of the aged – and some young – gardeners is to have a totally labour-saving garden, but such is an illusion.

Further Reading

Below are details of publications mentioned in the book.

Arnold-Forster, W. (1948), *Shrubs for the Milder Counties*. London: Country Life. 2nd edn Penzance: Alison Hodge, 2000.

Brent, M., 'Palms', in McMillan Browse, P. (ed) (2004), *Gardening on the Edge*. Penzance: Alison Hodge, p. 87.

Fish, M. (1956), *We Made a Garden*. London: Collingridge.

Hadfield, M. (1960), *History of British Gardening*. London: Spring Books.

Haworth-Booth, M. (1951), *Effective Flowering Shrubs*. London: Collins.

Kelway, C. (1962), *Seaside Gardening*. London: Collingridge.

Paton, J.A. & Paton V.S. (2001), *Magnolias in Cornish Gardens*. Fowey: Alexander Associates.

Pett, D.E. (2003), *The Cornwall Gardens Guide*. Penzance: Alison Hodge.

Verey, R. (1981), *The Scented Garden*. London: Michael Joseph.

Verey, R. & Lawson, A. (1990), *Good Planting*. London: Frances Lincoln.

Vincent, C. (2003), *Concrete Works*. Penzance: Alison Hodge.

The Cornish Garden: Journal of the Cornwall Garden Society.

Acknowledgements

Photographs are reproduced by kind permission of: Angus Alexander, page 4 and cover (back flap); Viscount Boyd, page 44 (top); Freya Laughton: pages 32, 33, 35 (bottom), 36 (left), 37 (bottom right), cover; Michael Palmer, page 128 (top); Stephen Read, page 104 (top); the *Western Morning News*, page 26 (top). All other photographs are by the author.

First published in 2005 by
Alison Hodge
Bosulval, Newmill, Penzance, Cornwall TR20 8XA
info@alison-hodge.co.uk www.alison-hodge.co.uk

ISBN-13 978 0906720 41 9
ISBN-10 0 906720 41 9

British Library Cataloguing-in-Publication Data
A catalogue record for this book is available from the British Library.

Cover designed by Christopher Laughton

Designed and originated by
BDP – Book Development and Production,
Penzance, Cornwall

Printed in Singapore